W9-ASC-193

Jackie Robinson
and the
Integration of Baseball

Lucent Library of Black History

John F. Wukovits

LUCENT BOOKS

An imprint of Thomson Gale, a part of The Thomson Corporation

THOMSON

GALE

Detroit • New York • San Francisco
New Haven, Conn. • Waterville, Maine • London

For more information, contact
Lucent Books
27500 Drake Rd.
Farmington Hills, MI 48331-3535
Or you can visit our Internet site at http://www.gale.com

LIBRARY OF CONGRESS CATALOGING-IN-PUBLICATION DATA

Wukovits, John F. 1944–
   Jackie Robinson and the integration of baseball / by John F. Wukovits.
    p. cm.—(The lucent library of Black history) Includes bibliographical references and index.
   ISBN-13: 978-1-59018-913-9 (hard cover : alk. paper)
   ISBN-10: 1-59018-913-2 (hard cover : alk. paper)
  1. Robinson, Jackie, 1919-1972. 2. Baseball players—United States—Biography.
3. Discrimination in sports—United States—History. I. Title. II. Series.
GV865.R6W85
2006796.357092—dc22

                                               2006010831

Contents

Foreword

It has been more than 500 years since Africans were first brought to the New World in shackles, and over 140 years since slavery was formally abolished in the United States. Over 50 years have passed since the fallacy of "separate but equal" was obliterated in the American courts, and some 40 years since the watershed Civil Rights Act of 1965 guaranteed the rights and liberties of all Americans, especially those of color. Over time, these changes have become celebrated landmarks in American history. In the twenty-first century, African American men and women are politicians, judges, diplomats, professors, deans, doctors, artists, athletes, business owners, and home owners. For many, the scars of the past have melted away in the opportunities that have been found in contemporary society. Observers such as Peter N. Kirsanow, who sits on the U.S. Commission of Civil Rights, point to these accomplishments and conclude, "The growing black middle class may be viewed as proof that most of the civil rights battles have been won."

In spite of these legal victories, however, prejudice and inequality have persisted in American society. In 2003, African Americans comprised just 12 percent of the nation's population, yet accounted for 44 percent of its prison inmates and 24 percent of its poor. Racially motivated hate crimes continue to appear on the pages of major newspapers in many American cities. Furthermore, many African Americans still experience either overt or muted racism in their daily lives. A 1996 study undertaken by Professor Nancy Krieger of the Harvard School of Public Health, for example, found that 80 percent of the African American participants reported having experienced racial discrimination in one or more settings, including at work or school, applying for housing and medical care, from the police or in the courts, and on the street or in a public setting.

It is for these reasons that many believe the struggle for racial equality and justice is far from over. These episodes of discrimi-

nation threaten to shatter the illusion that America has completely overcome its racist past, causing many black Americans
to become increasingly frustrated and confused. Scholar and
writer Ellis Cose has described this splintered state in the following way: "I have done everything I was supposed to do. I have
stayed out of trouble with the law, gone to the right schools, and
worked myself nearly to death. What more do they want? Why
in God's name won't they accept me as a full human being?" For
Cose and others, the struggle for equality and justice has yet to
be fully achieved.

In many subtle yet important ways the traumatic experiences
of slavery and segregation continue to inform the way race is discussed and experienced in the twenty-first century. Indeed, it is
possible that America will always grapple with the fallout from
its distressing past. Ulric Haynes, dean of the Hofstra University
School of Business has said, "Perhaps race will always matter,
given the historical circumstances under which we came to this
country." But studying this past and understanding how it con-
tributes to present-day dialogues about race and history in America is a critical component of contemporary education. To this
end, the Lucent Library of Black History offers a thorough look
at the experiences that have shaped the black community and
the American people as a whole. Annotated bibliographies provide readers with ideas for further research, while fully docu-
mented primary and secondary source quotations enhance the
text. Each book in the series explores a different episode of black
history; together they provide students with a wealth of information as well as launching points for further study and discussion.

"All We Ask Is to Be Treated Fairly"

The eight-year-old Jackie Robinson just wanted to fulfill his mother's simple request. She had asked him to sweep the sidewalk. This was not an unusual request in the modest Pasadena, California, neighborhood where he lived—or in any community for that matter. What is more natural than a child completing chores for his parent?

But this was 1927, not 2006. And this was an African American youth sweeping the sidewalk in an all-white neighborhood into which his family had recently moved. It inevitably led to a clash.

"Nigger, nigger, nigger boy," shouted a young white girl from across the street as Robinson tidied the walk. In retaliation, Robinson yelled back that her father was "nothing but a cracker," a derogatory term applied to poor whites.

"Soda cracker's good to eat, nigger's only good to beat,"[1] chanted the girl in a rhythmic pattern. In a few moments she called to her father, who rushed outside and threw rocks at Jackie. The man only halted when his wife forced him to stop arguing with`a child.

The same year, Negro League first baseman George Giles started his baseball career barnstorming around the nation with a black all-star squad. The team traveled from city to city, competing against white squads that often contained major league stars. Giles endured abuse from the fans, not because he struck out at the plate or mishandled a play, but because of his skin color.

"Abilene [Kansas]! Never will forget it," Giles explained later.

> Went out to play an exhibition game, and I never heard the expression nigger used so much in my life. It was "nigger this" and "nigger that," and "look at that nigger run." I told the manager, "Man, let's hurry up and get this game over with so we can get out of town, 'cause I'm tired of hearing this word nigger." That was the way it was all over the country. See, we played all the states. Colorado was just as bad as Mississippi. New York was just as bad as Alabama. It was all the same.[2]

These two incidents—the taunting of a young Jackie Robinson and the experience of an older George Giles—illustrate the sad state of race relations in America in the first half of the twentieth century. This was a part of life that Jackie Robinson would help alter through his exploits on the baseball diamond. Few facets of daily life were untouched by segregation, an arrangement under which blacks and whites occupied separate worlds. Men, women, and children suffered from a system that used skin color to determine who should benefit from America's riches and who should not.

Segregated Baseball

That sentiment extended to the baseball field as well, where, mirroring society at large, two separate games existed: one for black professionals and one for whites. This segregation had not always existed. In baseball's early years black athletes played alongside whites. For example, teams from the East and Midwest commonly fielded integrated squads before the Civil War. In 1884 Moses Fleetwood ("Fleet") Walker became the first African American to play major league baseball when his Toledo, Ohio, minor league squad joined the American Association, at the time considered a major league. His presence in the lineup led to protests by white players on other teams, but a precedent had been established for both races to participate in top-flight baseball.

Eventually, though, strong opposition from whites to competing with blacks led to segregated baseball. On July 14, 1887, one of baseball's white legends, player-manager Cap Anson, refused to field his Chicago White Stockings against the Newark Little

Baseball legend Cap Anson, shown here in 1876, would not allow his Chicago White Stockings team to play against black ballplayers.

Giants unless Newark benched its two stars, black players George Washington Stovey and Fleet Walker. Newark, eager to play the game, caved in to Anson's demands.

That same day, the ten teams composing the International League met in Buffalo, New York, to discuss the issue of black athletes in the league. Worried that they would lose some of their top white players because of their animosity toward blacks, the teams voted to exclude blacks from future play. With that decision, a color line had been drawn. Team owners operated under an unwritten but clearly understood rule to assemble white-only squads.

With access to major league baseball denied, black athletes turned to two alternatives to showcase their talents. Barnstorming, which provided the main source of livelihood, pitted teams of African Americans against the best local talent during tours that crisscrossed the nation. The second alternative, all-black league play, pitted a set number of teams against each other in regularly scheduled games, much as is done today.

"Somebody Has to Make the First Move"

In halting steps over the years, a handful of individuals and organizations resisted segregation in baseball. Walter S. Brown, a black businessman in Baltimore who served as president of the National Colored League, said in 1887, "All we ask is to be treated fairly and given only half a chance and we will prove to the public that colored men are great ball players and give satisfaction to the entire public."[3]

In 1912 the *St. Louis Post-Dispatch*, one of the most influential white-owned publications in the nation, wrote of the predicament facing organized baseball and issued what, for those times, was an amazing statement in support of the black athlete. "[We wonder] if baseball is, after all, the great American game. We play it, to be sure, but the colored people play it so much better that the time is apparently coming when it shall be known as the great African game."[4]

The *Newark Call*, a black newspaper, disagreed with the color barrier and published persuasive arguments for why the inequality should end.

If anywhere in this world the social barriers are broken down it is on the ball field. There many men of low birth

The newspaper writer and columnist Heywood Broun denounced segregation in baseball.

and poor breeding are the idols of the rich and cultured: the best man is he who plays best. Even men of churlish dispositions and coarse hues are tolerated on the field. In view of these facts the objection to colored men is ridiculous.[5]

A group of white sportswriters and ball players promoted integration as early as the 1930s. Westbrook Pegler wrote in 1935 of "the silly unwritten law that bars dark Babe Ruths and [Dizzy] Deans from the money they deserve."[6] Heywood Broun and Shirley Povich, two other respected white newspaper writers, also condemned the exclusion of blacks.

In 1937 the owner of the Pittsburgh Pirates, William Benswanger, then involved in a heated race for the pennant, gushed in a newspaper article how pleasant his team's prospects would be if some of the top black players played for him. "If [the race question] came to an issue, I'd vote for Negro players. I know there are many problems connected with the question, but after all, somebody has to make the first move."[7]

It would be another ten years before Benswanger's dream would come true. Until then, black ball players continued to endure the indignities that had made their athletic lives so arduous. In 1947 one man, aided by a small handful of others, changed that and much more. By smashing the color barrier that existed in major league baseball, Jackie Robinson gave hope to millions of African Americans, both inside and outside the sporting world, that life could one day be better. His courageous actions in the smaller arena of baseball helped fuel the drive for equality in society at large.

"A life is not important, except in the impact it has on other lives,"[8] Jackie Robinson stated. Not often does an individual live up to his own words, but in more ways than one, Jackie Robinson proved the truth of his statement.

Chapter One

"You Watched the White Kids Splash Around"

Two strong personalities, both female, helped shape Jackie Robinson. His maternal grandmother, Edna McGriff, maintained her dignity even though she spent the early portions of her life laboring as a slave on a plantation. She suffered the abuses of the slave system that existed until the mid-1800s and endured the continuing bigotry that followed slavery's abolition, but she mentally bowed to no individual. McGriff, who seemed to contain the history of her beleaguered race in a face that "had a thousand wrinkles in it,"[9] made a point to tell her grandson that he had a self-respect and worth that only he could take away by acting as less than a man.

McGriff passed down her strengths to her daughter, Mallie, a deeply religious individual who believed that hard work led to a better life. Mallie married Jerry Robinson on November 21, 1909, and moved into a cabin on a Georgia plantation owned by Jim Sasser, a white businessman. In exchange for toiling in Sasser's fields, Robinson received $12 a month and the right to inhabit the cabin. But Mallie soon became disenchanted with an arrangement that would, by her account, keep them in a perpetual state of poverty. She encouraged her husband, who was one of the hardest-working men in the fields, to seek a better deal with Sasser. Instead of the monthly wage, Robinson asked to be a sharecropper—Sasser would provide the housing, land, and fertilizer for Robinson, who would then share half of his crops with Sasser. A hesitant Sasser only agreed to the deal to avoid losing his best worker, but he realized who the inspiration was behind the scenes. Using language common for the times, he told Mallie, "You're about the sassiest nigger woman ever on this place."[10]

"He Had No Right to Desert"

Fueled by Jerry's hard work and Mallie's grit, the young couple slowly improved their standard of living. They earned an income in town selling the produce they grew, money that was dearly needed for their growing family. Between 1910 and 1916 they had four children—Edgar born in 1910, Frank born in 1911, Mack born in 1914, and Willa Mae born in 1916.

Their last child, Jackie Roosevelt Robinson, was born on January 31, 1919, in Cairo, Georgia, a small community a few miles north of the Florida state line. Named partly after Theodore Roosevelt, a renowned American president who opposed racism, Jackie resided in one of Georgia's most impoverished areas.

A photograph taken about 1925 shows future Hall of Famer Jackie Robinson as a young boy.

Slavery had been abolished more than half a century earlier, but a residue of hatred continued in the practices that dominated Southern life. In the nine years before Robinson's birth, 125 blacks had been lynched in Georgia. The state's most important city, Atlanta, had been the scene of a violent racial riot in 1906, when whites killed four prominent black citizens in the midst of burning and looting black businesses. The white supremacist group, the Ku Klux Klan, was active in Georgia, and only three months before

Jackie's birth, whites killed five blacks and burned seven black churches in retaliation for the death of two white Georgia policemen. Mallie chafed at the restrictions she faced in the segregated society, but she endured them as long as she had a family and a husband.

That changed six months after Jackie's birth, however, when Jerry Robinson told Mallie he had to travel to Texas to visit his brother. The story was a ruse to cover the fact that he was leaving with another woman, and Mallie never again saw her husband.

Now abandoned with five small children, Mallie faced an uncertain future. When Jim Sasser learned that the farmland occupied by the Robinson family now had no man to work it, he moved Mallie and the children to smaller quarters on poorer land. Without an income, and no longer living on productive soil, Mallie had to take whatever odd jobs around town that she could find.

"Later, when I became aware of how much my mother had to endure alone, I could only think of him [his father] with bitterness," Robinson wrote in his autobiography. "He, too, may have been a victim of oppression, but he had no right to desert my mother and five children."[11]

Throughout her ordeal, Mallie's half-brother, Burton Thomas, urged her to uproot and join him in Pasadena, California. "If you poor Georgia folks want to get a little closer to heaven, come on out to California,"[12] Thomas repeated. Unable to fend for her family, in 1920 thirty-year-old Mallie Robinson took her half-brother's advice and made plans to travel west.

"There's No Law Against Skating, Is There?"

In May, Robinson gathered her children, ages nine to one, and boarded a train bound for California. Not allowed to mingle with the white passengers, the six sat in the segregated cars on uncomfortable wooden seats as the train crossed west from Georgia to California. When they arrived in Pasadena, they lived for a brief time with Thomas, but the crowded conditions and lack of privacy sharing a home with others prodded Robinson to move her family out as soon as possible. When she had saved enough from the money earned at various cleaning and ironing jobs, Robinson and a relative purchased a home in an all-white neigh-

The Robinson family poses for a portrait in 1925. Seated is Mallie Robinson. The children (from left to right) are Mack, Jackie, Edgar, Willa Mae, and Frank.

borhood on Pepper Street in Pasadena and moved the family out of Thomas's home.

Robinson continued to work long hours to ensure that her children had a roof over their heads. She often awoke before dawn and did not return until after dark, but even that failed to support their needs. On the worst days, she could feed her children only bread and water. "Sometimes there were only two meals a day," Jackie Robinson recalled in his autobiography, "and some days we wouldn't have eaten at all if it hadn't been for the leftovers my mother was able to bring home from her job."[13]

Swallowing her pride, Jackie's mother applied for welfare as a way of supplementing whatever money she brought home after cleaning and washing other people's homes and clothes. Gradually, she fashioned a stable existence for her sons and daughter. They enjoyed the bounties produced by the apple, orange, peach,

Pepper Street Gang

---◼---

Though Jackie Robinson and the companions who composed the Pepper Street Gang were far from hardcore juvenile delinquents, they did land in trouble often enough to make their names known to the local police. As Robinson related in *Wait Till Next Year*, one of the gang's favorite stunts was to sit on curbs and toss dirt clods at passing automobiles. They continued this activity until a police car showed up, at which time the boys split in different directions. The police never caught the speedy Robinson, but sometimes they were able to track down one of the slower boys. If that happened, the Robinsons invariably heard a knock on their front door from a uniformed officer, and Jackie had some hard explaining to do.

and fig trees that dotted their yard, and they so enjoyed the five-bedroom, two-bathroom home that they started calling it the "Castle."

They may have lived in what they termed a castle, but bigotry ruled the kingdom. Shortly after they moved in, Mallie asked Edgar to put on his roller skates and head to the store for a loaf of bread. A policeman appeared at their doorstep moments after Edgar returned, stating that the neighbors had complained about the noise Edgar made on his roller skates.

Mallie knew the real reason for the complaints, but maintained her composure. "I'm sorry they're so touchy that the noise of skates disturbs them," she said to the policeman. "But there's no law against skating on the sidewalk, is there?"

"No," replied the officer, "but the man who called us told us that his wife is afraid of colored people."[14]

Prejudice appeared in other ways: Someone burned a cross in their front lawn as a warning that blacks were not welcome; neighbors phoned complaints to the police that the Robinson children acted unruly. Instead of hiding from the threats, Mallie insisted on maintaining her normal schedule and refused to allow a handful of bigoted white neighbors to ruin her new life.

The situation came to a head when neighbors passed around a petition demanding the family move out of Pepper Street. Some white residents even discussed trying to purchase the Robinson home to speed the family's departure. The only white person on the street with enough money to do so, Clara Coppersmith, lived next door to the Robinsons, and she declined to go along. Edgar had chopped wood and done other chores for her without accepting money, and now she repaid the kindness.

Mallie Robinson's Dignified Response

Thus blunted in their attempt to force the Robinsons out of their home, the neighbors sat back and waited for another opportunity. Robinson, however, intended to win them over with kindness, respect, and pride. She had stressed to her children the importance of religion, family, self-discipline, kindness, and education. Though she could be firm-handed when needed, and even turn to a spanking on occasion, Robinson relied more on discussions with her children whenever a problem arose. She would take the same quiet approach with the neighbors.

Believing that the best way to receive kindness was to first give it, Robinson opened her home to her neighbors. Every Saturday evening, a local bakery owner allowed the boys to cart away whatever bread and baked goods he had left over, and the milkman often shared his excess product with the family. Robinson suddenly had more than her family could handle, so she let word spread that any of the neighbors were welcome to come over and help themselves to the produce. White residents reacted warily at first, not knowing what to expect, but once one person walked up the front steps and knocked on the Robinsons' door, the walls of separation began gradually to disappear.

Neighbors marveled, "Their [the Robinsons'] door was never locked. You could go in any time, day or night, help yourself to anything in the kitchen—everybody in the neighborhood knew that."[15] Daughter Willa Mae recalled, "And then we got to be real friends and all in the neighborhood. They found out we were human, too; the color didn't do anything to them."[16]

Mallie Robinson did not merely instruct her children to be friendly and fair to others—she lived it. Jackie grew up in the presence of a strong woman who gave respect and insisted on being respected in turn. "I remember, even as a small boy, having a lot of pride in my mother,"[17] he wrote later in life.

Influences Mold Robinson

Jackie started seeing a different world once he entered the structured realm of education, where he mingled with other children and with teachers. Many of the instructors in those days reflected the prejudices of society, but Jackie's kindergarten and first grade teachers, Miss Gilbert and Miss Haney, treated him with decency. In the earlier days of the family living in California, before his mother's financial situation had improved, the teachers sometimes handed sandwiches to Jackie when they knew he had had little to eat before coming to school.

Jackie entered Washington Junior High in 1931. He earned mainly B's and C's throughout his school years. His transcript from Washington Junior High reflected mostly average grades. It also showed attitudes toward African Americans. At one point during his years in school, a counselor wrote that Jackie's future occupation would probably be no more exalted than that of a gardener.

Few seemed to notice the basketball or football that young Jackie carried with him through the neighborhood and school halls. Mathematics and history failed to ignite a spark, but a transformation occurred when Jackie donned a baseball glove or trotted onto a basketball court. The shy young man suddenly came alive.

He played his first competitive game in the fourth grade when he and his soccer teammates took the field. Jackie enjoyed the challenge of competition. He also enjoyed doing something in which race seemed unimportant. In sports, generally the better player or better team won. Unlike much of American society, the rules were not stacked in favor of or against an athlete because of skin color.

Jackie's interest quickly expanded to football, tennis, basketball, track, baseball, and even table tennis. He became so adept at every sport he tried that his classmates offered to share their lunches with Jackie if he agreed to play on their team. As soon as school ended, Jackie rushed home, dropped off his school books, and headed to the closest field or court.

Despite the wholesome nature of his pastime pursuits, young Robinson narrowly avoided trouble. For a brief time, Jackie was an active member of the Pepper Street Gang, a group of poor black, Japanese, and Mexican youths. The gang did a lot of stupid things like throwing rocks at street lights, stealing fruit, and

Duke Snider

■

Two individuals who grew up in the same California region wound up as teammates years later. Born in Los Angeles, California, on September 19, 1926, Edward Donald "Duke" Snider joined the Brooklyn Dodgers in 1947, the same year Jackie Robinson broke the color barrier. The center fielder provided tremendous power for the Dodger lineup and smashed forty or more home runs in five consecutive years in the 1950s.

Coincidentally, after watching Jackie Robinson perform for Pasadena Junior College, Snider rose through the baseball ranks to become Robinson's teammate during the turbulent 1947 season. He competed in the majors from 1947 until his retirement in 1964, playing for the New York Mets and San Francisco Giants as well as for the Dodgers. The eight-time baseball all-star batted .295 for a career average and smacked 407 home runs, feats for which he was elected to the Baseball Hall of Fame in 1980.

Duke Snider clutches baseball bats in the Brooklyn Dodgers' locker room in 1952.

shoplifting candy bars. Though these were not serious offenses, their activities made them known to local police officers.

Fortunately for young Jackie Robinson, a handful of concerned adults stepped in to provide more positive influence. One was Captain Hugh D. Morgan, the head of the Youth Division in the Pasadena Police Department. Morgan had studied juvenile delinquency and lent advice and money to Jackie and other youths in hope of steering them along the right path. He suggested alternate ways to spend their time, such as sports, church, or jobs, and could usually find a dollar or two when any of the

Reflecting the segregation of the era, African American women stand outside a separate theater entrance for blacks in Florida in 1950.

youths needed money for food or shoes. Morgan tried to convey that a person could overcome difficult circumstances, including racism, by setting goals and working hard to attain them.

Carl Anderson, a local automobile mechanic, also took an interest in Jackie. Anderson urged Jackie to be his own person and find out what he wanted to do with his life rather than just follow the others. Anderson explained that it took more guts for a person to mark his own path than to go along with everybody else. The Reverend Karl Downs, pastor of the Robinsons' church, spent hours counseling Jackie and showing the importance of religion to him and other youths. As a result, when he was in high school Jackie started teaching Sunday school.

"You Stay Out of Those Neighborhoods"

The help and guidance from these men bolstered that given by his mother and helped him overcome difficult conditions. Life for blacks in California was better than in Georgia. Jackie attended an integrated school and lived in a mostly white neighborhood, for example. But in numerous ways, Jackie knew that whites considered him inferior. When he attended a movie, Jackie and the other blacks had to sit in the balcony rather than on the main floor. Blacks could only use the city's swimming pool one day a week—after which workers drained and cleaned the pool. Jackie recalled watching from outside on humid summer days while the white children enjoyed the pool, but he could not enter the area. "During hot spells, you waited outside the picket fence and watched the white kids splash around,"[18] he said. Jackie suffered with the knowledge that other children thought he was inferior because he was darker-skinned than they were.

Discrimination surfaced often and in many different settings. One time Jackie and his buddies jumped into the town's reservoir for a swim. Admittedly the group had broken a law by sneaking into the area's water supply, but the official reaction overshadowed the offense. As the boys swam, they were interrupted by a gruff voice proclaiming, "Looka there—niggers swimming in my drinking water!" The sheriff and his deputies arrested the group and detained them in jail for four hours. When one of the boys complained of hunger, the sheriff said to a deputy, "The coon's hungry. Go buy a watermelon."[19] When the deputy returned with the watermelon, the police snapped photographs of the group devouring the food.

Though the Supreme Court had ruled in 1917 that cities could not restrict minority housing to certain zones of town, unofficial segregation still existed. One of Jackie's junior high classmates, Yoshi Hasagawa, said, "There weren't signs in the neighborhoods or anything [indicating an all-white neighborhood], but you didn't need them. If you were black or Japanese or Mexican, you just made it a point to stay out of those neighborhoods."[20] Such attitudes meant that Jackie could feel safe on Pepper Street, whose white residents had grudgingly accepted him and his family, but he could not feel free to walk wherever he wanted. A stroll by a black person into a white enclave might result in derogatory remarks or even violence.

Mallie Robinson continued to insist that her children react to racism with calm dignity. As her sons grew into the teenage years, they sometimes ignored her advice. Mack, especially, never backed down from a fight, sometimes joined by his brothers. "Kids aren't so tough when you can knock them down with a punch,"[21] Mack later explained.

The Will to Win

If his brothers proved that they could hold their own in a fight, Jackie showed on the athletic field that he was someone to be respected. He attended John Muir Technical High School, which had a reputation for its top-caliber athletic teams. As he had in his junior high school years, Jackie became a standout player in football, basketball, baseball, and track.

"Robinson was all over the [basketball] floor," stated one local newspaper of a recent contest, "and when he wasn't scoring points he was making impossible 'saves' and interceptions, and was the best player on the floor."[22] As a senior in 1938, in one outstanding day Jackie set a new running broad jump record in the morning in one town, then drove to a second city in the afternoon to help the school's baseball team win the league championship.

Jackie excelled at each sport because, in addition to his pure athleticism, he detested losing. His determination to win even irritated a few teammates, who thought he carried it too far. "He took losses very hard," said one teammate. "The rest of us might shrug off a loss, but Jack would cry if we lost."[23]

Jackie Robinson is shown here in 1941 during his days as a basketball player for UCLA.

By the end of his high school career, Jackie had batted over .400 in baseball, won track competitions, and was the key player in both basketball and football. The Pasadena *Star-News* named Jackie as Muir's most outstanding athlete.

Jackie Robinson's athletic prowess, however, would soon prove more than just an opportunity to gain him respect. It would provide him a chance to get a college education, first at a local junior college and then at one of the nation's most prestigious universities.

Chapter Two

Trying to Fit In

In the summer of 1937 Jackie Robinson, by now standing just under six feet tall and weighing only 135 pounds, enrolled at Pasadena Junior College. Attending college represented a chance to escape the racism practiced routinely in America at the time. The school opened all classes and facilities to any student, regardless of race. Still, blacks composed a miniscule percentage of the four-thousand-strong student body. No more than seventy blacks attended at the time.

Robinson's shyness made forming friendships difficult. One classmate, Jack Gordon, said that Robinson at first preferred to quietly observe his fellow students rather than introduce himself to others. Downs, who told Robinson that every person had to battle for equality and to stand up for his rights, helped the young man to become more self-confident. As Robinson's confidence grew, he began to urge his fellow black students to sit toward the front of the lecture hall rather than linger in the rear of the room. This, he believed, would be a way of asserting their right to learn as equals of white students. His activities drew the attention of both white and black students, who responded by electing Robinson to the Lancers, a group of respected students who organized student activities.

Off campus, Robinson similarly refused to tolerate abuse from whites. While riding as a passenger in a car with a few black friends, Robinson heard a white motorist use a racial slur as he drove by. The driver of Robinson's car caught up with the offending motorist, and when he pulled over they stepped out and a brawl ensued. The police quickly descended on the scene and hauled away Robinson and his companions. When Pasadena Junior College's baseball coach learned that his star player was in jail, he asked, "What the hell is Jack doing this time? What's he in jail for?"[24] With his coach's aid, Robinson was released the following morning and the incident ended without charges being filed.

"Gift from Heaven"

Though Jackie Robinson's efforts against social injustice gained him some notice during his collegiate years, it was his sports accomplishments that enhanced his reputation around Pasadena. In two years at Pasadena Junior College, he was the top player on a football team that lost only two games, he was the basketball squad's leading scorer, and he helped corral a championship for the baseball team. He also shattered the national junior college amateur record in the broad jump—which just happened to have been held by his brother Mack.

Few athletes so deftly moved from one sport to another as did Robinson in his college years. "Five or six of us kids saw him play a baseball game," said eventual Hall of Fame baseball star Duke Snider, "leave in the middle of it with his uniform still on to trot over to compete in the broad jump in a track meet, and then run back and finish the baseball game just as if nothing unusual had happened."[25]

In the fall of 1938 he led the Pasadena football team to an undefeated 11-0 record and the junior college championship, scoring 131 points and gaining more than 1,000 yards running. In the season opener he returned a punt 83 yards for a touchdown. In a game against San Bernardino Junior College he ran for three touchdowns and passed for another three scores. He kicked field goals in other contests. Duke Snider remembered watching in amazement during one football game when Robinson fielded a kickoff, reversed field three times, and wove through the opposing eleven defenders to score a touchdown. His performances led coach Tom Mallory to label Robinson his "Gift from Heaven."[26]

In 1937 Mack Robinson breaks the national junior college amateur broad jump record, which younger brother Jackie would later beat.

Robinson displayed similar daring on the baseball field, where he routinely got to first base and then garnered scoring opportunities with his ability to steal bases. He stole so often and so easily that a sportswriter wrote, "It's practically a habit. That isn't stealing. It's grand larceny."[27]

Robinson later recalled that at this time, baseball was not his main focus because the game was so rigidly segregated. He loved every sport, but,

Like most Negro athletes, I just assumed that baseball was a sport without a professional future. I played it solely for the fun of it. Football, on the other hand, held out some kind of a future. Professional teams in the Pacific Coast Leagues did not discriminate against Negro players. The same was true of basketball. There were any number of professional teams made up of both whites and Negroes.[28]

"Jack Would Not Take Any Stuff"

For all of Jackie Robinson's obvious talent, sports reflected the inequalities American society imposed on blacks. He gained adulation among fans by scoring touchdowns or stealing second base, but he also could not help noticing the racial slurs and actions directed at him. For example, when Robinson first appeared for the Pasadena Junior College football team in the late summer of 1937, a group of white teammates, all from Oklahoma, threatened to quit the team unless Jackie was dismissed. Coach Mallory put a speedy end to the uprising by telling them that Robinson was their teammate, and if they did not like it they could leave the team. The players' opposition crumbled in the face of their coach's refusal to tolerate racism. Robinson absorbed this lesson in the value of taking an unpopular stand.

"Freedom of Choice"

Jackie Robinson was a complex individual, but his desire for the future was quite simple. He wanted to be treated as any other man—with respect—and he would treat others with the same respect. He stated this belief in his 1972 autobiography, *I Never Had It Made*.

The first freedom for all people is freedom of choice. I want to live in a neighborhood of my choice where I can afford to pay the rent. I want to send my children to school where I believe they will develop best. I want the freedom to rise as high in my career as my ability indicates. I want to be free to follow the dictates of my own mind and conscience without being subject to the pressures of any man, black or white.

Jackie Robinson, as told to Alfred Duckett, *I Never Had It Made*. New York: G.P. Putnam's Sons, 1972, p. 115.

More difficult to overcome was the racism practiced by people in other parts of the country. In his second year the team traveled to Phoenix, Arizona, for a game. Robinson and three other black players were told they could not stay at the same hotel as their white teammates. Shown the poor accommodations reserved for them, the four sat all night in the lobby of their teammates' hotel rather than endure the indignity of such inferior conditions.

During games, Robinson received more abuse than the other black players. Opponents on the court or field targeted him, but Robinson refused to knuckle under. If a pitcher aimed the baseball at his head, forcing him to dive out of the way, Robinson would dust himself off and jump right back into the batter's box to make it clear he had not been intimidated. In one memorable basketball game, a Long Beach State guard kept thrusting his hands and fingers into Robinson's face and mouth. Finally, Robinson bit the player, an action that produced a near riot but informed the opponent that Jackie Robinson was to be respected.

Refusing to Let Emotions Rule

Off the basketball court or the ball field, Robinson was equally insistent on being treated with respect. He did not engage in fighting very often but would if he felt he needed to. A reporter wrote in the student paper,

> They [the police] didn't regard Jack as a rabble-rouser. Not at all. It's just that Jack would not take any stuff from them [opponents who resorted to racial slurs], and they knew it. Frankly, some of them were bigots then. Jack never wanted to be regarded as a second-class citizen. He rebelled at any thought of anybody putting him down, or putting any of his people down. He wanted equality.

The reporter added that Robinson refused to let emotions rule his temper. "When he felt he was right and the other guy was wrong, he didn't hesitate."[29]

By the end of his second year at Pasadena Junior College, Robinson had drawn the attention of people outside of college, including professional baseball teams. In March 1938 he was part of a group of Pasadena players chosen to compete against the Chicago White Sox for an exhibition game during spring training. Robinson performed so well against the major leaguers—two hits, a stolen base, and a nifty execution on a double play ball—that the White Sox manager, Jimmy Dykes, muttered afterward, "Geez, if that kid was white I'd sign him right now."[30]

Although major league baseball was still closed to blacks, Robinson had numerous offers from acclaimed universities. Since his brother Frank was such an avid fan of his, Robinson decided to remain close to home. He accepted a scholarship from UCLA (University of California at Los Angeles) to play football and baseball for the school's teams, known as the Bruins.

Happy Times

The University of California suited the young athlete just fine. "Those were happy days at UCLA," Robinson recalled. "I was a college star, a campus hero—the height of most American boys' ambition." He added, "It seemed I could never get enough of games and sports."[31]

Robinson (center) enjoyed his time at UCLA, where he played football with fellow Gold Dust Trio members Woody Strode (left) and Kenny Washington.

After a stellar sports career at Pasadena Junior College, Robinson added to his laurels at UCLA. In the fall of 1939 he teamed at quarterback with halfback Kenny Washington and receiver Woody Strode to form what the press labeled the Gold Dust Trio and led the Bruins to an undefeated season. One opposing coach called Robinson the best backfield runner he had seen in twenty-five years of coaching. Yet Robinson found the Bruins' season a disappointment. A tie against archrival University of Southern California (USC) in the final regular season game kept the Bruins from going to the prestigious Rose Bowl game, played on New Year's Day. The failure to win outright so bothered Robinson that he ran into the showers after the game, turned on all the showers so no one could hear him, and broke down crying.

As the right forward on the basketball squad, Robinson displayed a deft touch in passing and shooting. Though the team failed to register a winning record, in 1940 Robinson led the league in scoring with more than eleven points per game, an accomplishment that led one rival coach to call him the best college basketball player in the nation.

As he had done at Pasadena Junior College, Robinson illustrated his diverse athletic talents by participating on the baseball and track teams. The baseball squad compiled a mediocre record, but Robinson won broad jump titles in both the Pacific Coast Conference meet and the National Collegiate Athletic Association national meet.

Robinson recalled later that his mother might have been happier had he devoted more energy to scholarship.

> My mother wanted me to concentrate on my studies. She wanted me to become a doctor, or a lawyer, or a coach. I wasn't interested in the first two, but I did like the coaching idea. It gave me an excuse to play games all the time. "If I'm going to be a coach," I'd tell her, "I'll have to keep playing. You can't teach a game if you don't know it."[32]

"He Was Never, Ever, Ashamed of His Color"

Robinson in fact did devote some of his energies to nonsporting activities, and he found these to be rewarding as well. In his two years at UCLA he worked part-time at Campbell's Book Store,

At a UCLA track meet in 1940 Robinson appears to fly through the air with this winning broad jump.

which catered to UCLA students. The white owners, Robert and Blanche Campbell, treated Robinson the same as all of the other employees, helping him realize that individuals could overcome prejudice and form lifelong friendships.

One other person made Robinson's time at UCLA memorable —in 1939 he met the young woman who would one day become his wife. Shy in the presence of women, Robinson was struck by Rachel Isum's looks but hesitated to introduce himself.

Isum had seen Robinson play football in high school, and though she never met him, she thought he was arrogant. She had noticed how he stood around in the backfield between plays with his hands on his hips. Isum interpreted Robinson's stance as a

Robinson (center) is stopped after receiving a pass during a 1939 football game at UCLA, where he lettered in four sports.

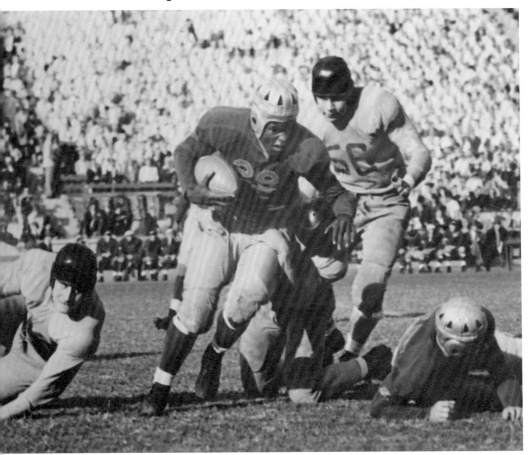

statement to spectators and opposing players that he was the star of the game.

It was Robinson's good friend and fellow student, Ray Bartlett, who introduced the pair to each other. After a few awkward moments of silence, Robinson and Isum began talking. Isum discovered that her first impressions had been inaccurate. Robinson's warm smile complemented an obvious pride in his being an African American. Isum noticed that Robinson's white shirts provided a stark contrast of colors that emphasized the blackness of his skin. "He wore his color with such dignity and pride and confidence that after a little while I didn't even think about it," Isum explained. "He wouldn't let me. He was never, ever, ashamed of his color."[33]

The two quickly became a couple and were always seen together around campus. Eventually, Robinson gave Isum a charm bracelet with miniature footballs, basketballs, and baseballs. Though not an official engagement ring, Robinson intended that the bracelet would symbolize their commitment to each other.

After the basketball season ended during his second year at UCLA, Robinson decided to leave in mid-year rather than remain in school until June and receive a college degree. His grades had never been that good. He earned mostly C's, and he argued that a college education would not help him attain what a white graduate would get—a high-paying job. Instead, he wanted to pursue a career in sports, possibly as a coach or working in a youth program, which at that time was a realistic goal even without a degree. Robinson also hoped to earn a few dollars playing baseball or football with semiprofessional teams. His mother and Downs tried to convince him to remain at UCLA, but the young man would not be persuaded.

"He Is the Jim Thorpe of His Race"

Robinson soon landed a job as a youth counselor for the National Youth Administration, a government agency that offered camps and other activities for young people. Robinson worked at a camp north of Los Angeles for a few months. Then government funds ran out and the place closed. Some other plan was needed.

Fortunately for Robinson, the sporting world offered the break he needed. Shortly after the camp closed, Robinson received an invitation to play in a football all-star game against the National Football League champion Chicago Bears. Though the professionals soundly thrashed the all-stars 37-13, Robinson impressed observers with his outstanding play, especially a pass he snared from Boston College's Charlie O'Rourke and took to the end zone.

One sportswriter, Vincent X. Flaherty, compared Robinson to the boxer, Joe Louis, who had two years earlier beaten a heavily favored white man in the 1936 Olympics.

> In the general uproar about Joe Louis and his universal appeal, the colored race has lost sight of Jackie Robinson, the UCLA phenomenon whom seasoned observers consider

An athletic contemporary of Jackie Robinson, the formidable heavyweight champion Joe Louis strikes a boxing pose in 1935.

Nurse Rachel

———————■———————

While Robinson was in the military, he and Rachel experienced a rocky relationship. Rachel wanted to join the Nurse Cadet Corps, a young women's organization loosely affiliated with the military, designed to treat wounded soldiers. She felt compelled to do something for the war effort, especially as her older brother was listed as missing in action after his plane was shot down in Europe. When she told Robinson, to whom she was at this point engaged, he opposed the move. Jackie did not want Rachel to be subject to the rigors of a military life. When he told her to either leave the Nurse Cadet Corps or end their engagement, Rachel mailed back the bracelet and ring he had given her.

The breakup did not last long. Shortly before leaving the army, Robinson returned home to visit his mother. She saw how miserable he was without Rachel and told him to contact her. When he did, the two patched things up.

the greatest colored athlete of all time. And where the less talented Joe Louis has reaped a financial harvest out of boxing, the future holds no such riches for Robinson, who studied physical education at UCLA and who intends to make his mark in coaching.

Flaherty went on to evoke another famed minority athlete, the Native American track and field sensation, Jim Thorpe.

So it is a shame, then, in this day when Joe Louis monopolizes the affection of the Negro sports public, that Robinson isn't equally appreciated, or more universally known. He has everything Joe Louis has and more as regards personality, intelligence and native talent. And although there may be another Joe Louis in boxing, the thought of another athlete such as Jackie Robinson appearing upon the scene seems utterly fantastic. He is the Jim Thorpe of his race.[34]

Had he been white, Robinson would have landed a plum job. Instead, he received meager offers from the Broadway Clowns, a semiprofessional basketball team, and from a Mexican baseball organization.

"Neither of us thought about sports as a living because it wasn't happening," explained Bartlett of the possibility of playing professional sports. "Actually we probably didn't talk much about the future because we weren't sure what it would be."[35]

In September 1941 Robinson and his former UCLA teammate Bartlett agreed to play football for the Honolulu Bears for one hundred dollars a game and the promise of a construction job. As Robinson headed toward Hawaii aboard the transport that fall of 1941, major league sports appeared closed to the young athlete. And Robinson had no way of knowing that before the end of the year, a war would make that dream even less attainable.

Chapter Three

"Too Bad He's the Wrong Color"

After completing his football season with the Honolulu Bears, Robinson decided to return to California rather than remain in Hawaii and work the construction job. On December 5, 1941, Robinson boarded a passenger liner to begin the ocean trip home to California.

Two days later while at sea, Robinson noticed the ship's crew suddenly painted the windows black, an unusual step for a vessel whose main purpose was pleasure and comfort. An announcement from the captain cleared up the mystery. He explained to the passengers that earlier in the day, the Japanese had unleashed a surprise attack against the American military installations in Pearl Harbor, Hawaii. The windows, he said, were being painted black to prevent light from cabins illuminating the ship at night and making it an easier target for Japanese submarines that might be lurking in the shipping lanes. Robinson had barely missed being in Hawaii when the Japanese attacked, but the start of war would alter his and everyone else's lives in the coming years. The country badly needed military personnel to meet the threat posed by Japan and Germany. Robinson and other African Americans stood to benefit, either with a role in the military or in a factory position vacated by a departing serviceman.

Into the Military

When Robinson returned to California he obtained a job in a Lockheed Aircraft factory. That lasted until April 3, 1942, when the local draft board ordered him to appear at the National Guard Armory in Pasadena to be processed into the military. The next month he headed to Fort Riley, Kansas, to start thirteen weeks of basic training, followed by additional training in unit maneuvers and command.

When he arrived at Fort Riley, Robinson quickly found that the army was segregated, with blacks and whites serving in separate units. Secretary of War Henry L. Stimson expressed the opinion held by many white officials that blacks were unfit for combat duty. "There is a consensus that colored units are inferior to the

Jackie Robinson was commissioned as a second lieutenant in the U.S. Army in 1943 while at Fort Riley, Kansas.

performance of white troops, except for service duties,"[36] stated one government memorandum. Black units were commanded by white officers, on the assumption that blacks lacked the ability to lead more than small numbers of men. "Leadership is not embedded in the negro race yet," stated Stimson, "and to try to make commissioned officers to lead men into battle—colored men—is only to work a disaster to both."[37]

Robinson soon proved that he was no more willing to put up with racism in the army than he was in civilian life. Hoping to assemble a football team that would beat teams from other army bases, an officer asked Robinson to play. When the young private learned that the officer intended to keep him benched in games against army posts in the South, however, he declined. "I said that I had no intention of playing football for a team which, because I was black, would not allow me to play in all the games." When the colonel told the young soldier that he could order him to play, Robinson answered that although he could be ordered to play, he could not be forced to do his best. "You wouldn't want me playing on your team, knowing that my heart wasn't in it,"[38] Jackie said. The officer dropped his request and Robinson played, but the incident did not win Robinson any friends among the officers at Fort Riley.

Second Lieutenant Robinson

A friend among the officers is what Robinson needed, for he hoped to obtain a commission as an officer. That friend appeared in the form of Joe Louis, the famed black boxing champion, who served at the post for a time. When the army turned down Robinson's request for officers' school in late 1942, Louis interceded. He called his colleague and fellow African American, Truman Gibson, an assistant secretary of war in Washington, D.C., in charge of investigating racial matters, and asked him to help. Gibson checked into the situation, found nothing to disqualify Robinson, and ordered the army to accept him into officers' school. In January 1943, after completing his training, Robinson was commissioned as a second lieutenant.

Being an officer accorded Robinson some authority, but he soon learned that whites were unprepared to accept him as a man. A few months after receiving his commission, Robinson walked over to the baseball field to try out for Fort Riley's team, but was quickly spurned. "I'll break up the team before I'll have a nigger on it,"[39] the officer in charge growled. Faced with such blatant racism by a fellow officer, Robinson could only stand in stunned silence for a few moments, then turn and walk away.

"Something Could Be Accomplished by Speaking Out"

He may have held his tongue at the baseball field, but Robinson took his officer's duties seriously. His specific assignment was to be morale officer, and part of his job was to look into complaints from black soldiers about their treatment at Fort Riley. One condition that especially irked black troops was the segregated seating at the post's canteen, where soldiers could purchase sodas, cigarettes, and other items. The canteen set aside only a few stools and tables for blacks, meaning that they always had to endure long waits before they could eat the snacks they had paid for.

Robinson called Major Hafner, the white officer who was responsible for maintaining order on the post, and argued that blacks should have more access to the canteen. The major replied that taking seats from white soldiers would only aggravate conditions. "Lieutenant Robinson," the major said, unaware that the man he was speaking with on the phone was black, "are you suggesting that we ought to mix the races at the post exchange and let these Negro troops sit where they please?"

Robinson's reply was direct: "That's exactly what I'm suggesting. When they get over into those battle areas nobody's going to separate any bullets and label them 'for white troops' and 'for colored troops.'"

"Well, let's be reasonable, Lieutenant Robinson," said Hafner. "Let me put it this way: how would you like to have your wife sitting next to a nigger?"[40]

Robinson exploded at the racial slur, shouting that the problem rested more with white soldiers and with the major than it did with black soldiers. After informing Hafner that he had been talking to a black officer, Robinson slammed down the phone.

Those who overheard the exchange could hardly believe that Robinson had spoken to a white officer in such a manner. Fortunately for Robinson, his immediate supervisor, a white colonel named Longley, heard the conversation and promised that he would write a letter suggesting a change in the canteen's seating arrangement. His letter led to improvements for blacks.

"I have always been grateful to Colonel Longley," wrote Robinson. "He proved to me that when people in authority take a stand, good can come out of it." Jackie also saw that the incident had a positive effect on the morale of his men, as it "made my men realize that something could be accomplished by speaking out, and I hoped they would be less resigned to unjust conditions."[41]

Into the Deep South

Not long after this incident, the army transferred Robinson to Camp Hood, an Army installation in Texas that served as the home base for the 761st Tank Battalion, a black unit. Traveling to the Deep South was an eye-opener for a young man accustomed to the relative freedom of Pasadena. When he arrived, Robinson first noticed the sparkling white concrete buildings, but the jeep

Robinson headed a platoon in the all-black 761st Tank Battalion at Camp Hood in Texas (shown in this aerial view from the 1940s).

in which he sat passed right by those comfortable-looking quarters and drove to a muddy gulley in which were pitched a line of dirty, tattered World War I–vintage tents around which buzzed swarms of mosquitoes. Outhouses dotted the camp, with signs indicating they were reserved for "White," "Colored," or "Mexican." That would be his home for the next few months.

Robinson was assigned to head a platoon of the 761st. He knew absolutely nothing about the armored vehicles his unit was supposed to care for, and he decided that honesty would work best for him. During his initial meeting with the men, he confessed his ignorance, then asked for their help. He gave free rein to run the platoon to a veteran sergeant, promising that he would only step in if the sergeant needed help obtaining supplies or maintaining discipline. The strategy worked. The sergeant and the men responded to Robinson's honesty and became known as one of Camp Hood's most efficient platoons.

Colonel Paul L. Bates, the 761st's commanding officer, impressed Robinson from the start. Although he was white, Bates enjoyed an immediate rapport with the black soldiers he led. Realizing that they would always be harshly judged by white units, Bates insisted that the men be perfect in everything they did, from marching to making their beds, from clean uniforms to polished boots. He hoped that in doing so his men could earn the respect, however grudging, of white platoons at Camp Hood.

"Get to the Back of the Bus"

Its preparations complete, the 761st was due to head to Europe and combat against the Germans. Robinson had one small hurdle to clear, however. Medical authorities wanted to check Robinson's ankle, which he had injured some years earlier. Robinson had to travel by bus to a hospital thirty miles from the base.

The bus made a series of stops before leaving the base, during which white passengers began filing on. Though segregation on buses had been banned on military bases, off base it was legal in much of the South. As was his practice, the driver ordered the blacks to move to the back of the bus to make room for the white passengers.

Robinson, wearing the uniform of the United States Army and ready to enter combat to defend his country, shouted back that he

Paul L. Bates

---◼---

Colonel Paul L. Bates passed away in 1995, but the association he formed with the 761st Tank Battalion continues beyond his death. In 1999 following the wishes of Bates's will, the board of trustees of McDaniel College in Westminster, Maryland, began administering the Paul L. Bates Memorial Scholarship Fund. The fund, which Bates established to honor the brave men he led in World War II, provides financial assistance for descendants of the 761st Tank Battalion who served from August 1944 through April 1945. Recipients must demonstrate financial need and must maintain a 2.0 grade point average.

The man who so boldly came to Jackie Robinson's defense during the war is now assisting another generation of African Americans.

As commanding officer of the 761st Tank Battalion, Colonel Paul L. Bates insisted on raising the bar for his black soldiers.

had a right to remain in the seat and would not budge. The two traded insults for a few moments as stunned whites, unaccustomed to witnessing a black act with such impudence, watched the affair unfold. Before the bus driver made his final stop at the camp, he left the bus and brought back his company's dispatcher.

"Is this the nigger who's causing all the trouble?"[42] demanded the dispatcher. Robinson asserted that the civilian had no authority on a government post, and about this time the military police arrived. They asked him to accompany them to see the officer in charge and explain what had happened.

Robinson's appearance before the officer, a white captain, went poorly. The captain's assistant kept interjecting her own remarks without allowing Robinson to reply. Finally Robinson told her he would explain the entire affair if only she gave him a chance to speak, but that only resulted in the captain accusing Robinson of insulting a woman.

The incident resulted in Robinson being charged with insubordination, disturbing the peace, and conduct unbecoming an officer. Bates, however, refused to sign the necessary documents, since he considered the charges against his soldier unfair. The commanding general, though, was determined to teach Robinson and other blacks a lesson. He transferred Robinson to another tank battalion, whose commander readily signed the papers.

The case went to trial, but by this time black newspapers and the National Association for the Advancement of Colored People (NAACP) had taken up Robinson's cause. With the help of Bates, whose strong testimony on Robinson's behalf impressed everyone in the courtroom, the lieutenant was acquitted of all charges. "Colonel Bates came to the court-martial and confirmed every conviction I had held that not only was he a decent man with a keen sense of justice," recalled Robinson, "but he had courage to speak out even at the risk of personal loss."[43] Robinson had again stood up to prejudice, and once again had seen what the bravery of a single individual could do to alter a situation.

Out of the Military

Before the trial wound to its conclusion, Robinson's unit had already headed to Europe. The army stated that it would send him overseas with a different unit, but only if he signed a waiver relieving the army of responsibility should he further injure his weakened ankles. Robinson refused. The bus incident had left him doubtful of the military's commitment to fairness, and he doubted he would ever serve under another man as decent as Bates.

In November 1944 Robinson received an honorable discharge from the army for medical reasons. Floating bone chips and chronic arthritis, caused by a 1937 injury at Pasadena Junior College and aggravated playing football in Hawaii four years later, were cited as the reason.

Having fulfilled his obligations to the military, Robinson accepted a job as head basketball coach at Sam Houston College, a black institution in Texas. That position was short-lived. Before the season ended, Robinson met Ted Alexander who, before entering the service, had pitched for the Kansas City Monarchs baseball team, one of the nation's most revered teams in what was known as the Negro League. Alexander told Robinson to contact the Monarchs, as they were always looking for good players. Robinson did, and in April 1945 he signed a contract to play baseball for four hundred dollars a month, a sum that, for its time, was quite attractive.

"You Guys Better Get Ready"

Robinson soon learned what, besides opposing pitchers' fastballs, he had to brave for his pay. Though Jackie had endured his share of bigoted remarks and incidents, life with the Monarchs showed him what other black athletes accepted just so they could play the sport they loved. "When I look back at what I had to go through in black baseball," he later recalled, "I can only marvel at the many black players who stuck it out for years in the Jim Crow leagues because they had nowhere else to go."[44] Dilapidated hotels reserved for blacks, inadequately maintained baseball fields, long trips by bus or car to the next game, and inexperienced, poorly trained umpires taxed everyone's patience.

Despite the adversity, Robinson reveled in the chance to play with some of baseball's legendary talents. He told his roommate, Sammie Haynes, that he knew he was not as good as most of the players, such as pitcher Satchel Paige or outfielder Cool Papa Bell, but that he hoped to learn from them.

Supported by the wisdom and skills of his teammates, Robinson enjoyed a great year. Official statistics were not kept at that time in black baseball, but according to anecdotal accounts, he batted almost .350 and stole numerous bases.

Despite such impressive numbers, Robinson, like most black athletes of the mid-1940s, remained anonymous to most white Americans. Still, scouts from the major leagues were watching. In April 1945 the Boston Red Sox, under pressure from a local politician to examine black talent, invited Robinson and three teammates to a tryout at Fenway Park. Robinson astounded observers with his batting skills. "I'm telling you," said Boston city councilman Isadore Muchnick, whose district included many black voters, "you never saw anyone hit The Wall [Fenway's notoriously high left field fence] the way Robinson did that day. Bang, bang, bang;

In 1945 Jackie Robinson wears the uniform of the Kansas City Monarchs, the renowned Negro League ball club.

The Segregationist Commissioner

Judge Kenesaw Mountain Landis had two loves in his life—the law and baseball. He had played the sport in high school and closely followed the exploits of star players. Landis became baseball commissioner shortly after the infamous 1919 World Series, in which a group of Chicago White Sox players rigged the outcome in return for money. Landis worked to repair the damage to the credibility of the game, done by what became known as the "Black Sox" scandal, by banning eight of the White Sox players from major league baseball. Over the decade that followed, Landis insisted on having his authority over major league baseball recognized by all who were involved in the sport.

Landis, however, was an avowed segregationist, and as long as he remained commissioner, he blocked attempts to integrate baseball. When

he died on November 25, 1944, the door inched open to Jackie Robinson and other black players. The next year Branch Rickey and Jackie Robinson met and made baseball history.

Baseball commissioner Kenesaw Mountain Landis throws out the first ball at a Yankees-Dodgers game in 1941.

he rattled it."[45] Boston players crowded the dugout to watch Robinson knock one pitch after another against the towering wall or over it, and the Red Sox top scout, Hugh Duffy, exclaimed, "What a ballplayer! Too bad he's the wrong color."[46] Still, because the Red Sox had arranged the tryout only to satisfy the councilman, Robinson's performance did not lead to a contract. His name, however, began to circulate among major leaguers.

As the season with the Monarchs unfolded, Jackie became disenchanted with some of his teammates. Robinson felt that they were too willing to accept segregation and that they were too satisfied with being a top team in an all-black league. He wanted more.

"Well," Jackie told his teammates, "you guys better get ready because pretty soon baseball's going to sign one of us."[47] The event, with him as the center of focus, would happen sooner than he realized.

Chapter Four

"Guts Not to Fight Back"

By the time of Robinson's tryout in Boston, forces that would eventually open major league baseball to black athletes had been at work for some years. As early as 1931, Westbrook Pegler, an influential newspaper columnist, had called for complete integration. Prominent black newspapers printed a continuous stream of editorials and articles, many by columnist Wendell Smith, in an effort to prod baseball into accepting black players. Furthermore, race riots in Detroit, Chicago, and New York had put the nation on alert that it could not much longer ignore the deplorable state of race relations. Finally, few people could justify preventing black athletes from playing major league baseball while at the same time asking them to risk their lives on the World War II battlefields.

Branch Rickey

The most vocal proponent of integration among major league executives was Branch Rickey, head of the Brooklyn Dodgers. Rickey had long felt that excluding blacks from major league baseball was morally wrong. He was determined that the Dodgers would be the first team to sign a black baseball player. Not only would the move, if successful, remedy what was to

Branch Rickey, seated in his office as general manager of the Brooklyn Dodgers, forever changed baseball by integrating the sport.

him an obvious wrong, but he could add to the Dodger club some of the best talent available anywhere—the stars of the Negro League. With an improved club, the Dodgers' profit margin would soar. Thus, from a mixture of idealism and profit motive, came the opening that Jackie Robinson had predicted would occur.

The Search

As Rickey sought the right athlete, Smith told him about Robinson's impressive tryout with the Red Sox and added that Rickey could find no better individual than the former UCLA star. Rickey sent three different scouts to watch Robinson play. Each attended a different game, and none knew that two other scouts also were carrying out the same mission. When the three scouts returned to Rickey's office with their reports, each agreed that Robinson was the man to fill Rickey's needs.

In August 1945 Rickey dispatched scout Clyde Sukeforth to meet Robinson in Chicago, Illinois. Rickey told the scout to keep the real purpose of the meeting confidential, as he did not want any other team to move in ahead of him or, even worse, have an executive from the Kansas City Monarchs attempt to block the departure of one of their star players. Sukeforth asked Robinson about his background, about the court-martial, and a host of other subjects, and liked what he heard from the young man. "The more I talked to him the more impressed I was with him, with his determination and intelligence and aggressiveness,"[48] recalled Sukeforth.

On August 28, 1945, Robinson walked into Rickey's New York office for the historic meeting, still thinking that he was to discuss playing for a new black baseball team. The Dodger executive welcomed Robinson, then stared at the ballplayer for what seemed an eternity. Robinson stared right back, as if trying to assert that he was Rickey's equal. "Oh, they were a pair, those two!" remembered Sukeforth of the meeting's opening moments. "I tell you, the air in that office was electric."[49]

Then Rickey explained the real reason for the meeting. "I think you can play in the major leagues. How do you feel about it?" A stunned Robinson hardly knew what to say. "My reactions seemed like some kind of weird mixture churning in a blender. I was thrilled, scared, and excited. I was incredulous. Most of all, I was speechless."[50]

"Guts Enough to Not Fight Back"

Before he could respond, Rickey leaned over in his chair and said he had to have exactly the right man to be the first to break baseball's color barrier. He added that he had thoroughly investigated Robinson before asking him in and found he was the right man. Rickey had one major request to make, however. Knowing that Robinson had had a few battles in college and in the military, Rickey told him that he would have to quietly accept, at least for a time, racial slurs and abuse. "We can't fight our way through this, Robinson. We've got no army. There's virtually nobody on our side. No owners, no umpires, very few newspapermen. And I'm afraid that many fans will be hostile. We'll be in a tough position. We can win only if we can convince the world that I'm doing this because you're a great ballplayer and a fine gentleman."[51]

Rickey then slowed down to emphasize each word of his next sentence. "Have you got the guts to play the game no matter what happens?"[52] Rickey explained that opposing pitchers would purposely throw at his head, that opposing baserunners would try to spike him with their cleats, and that opposing dugouts and fans in the stands would unleash a torrent of hateful words.

Robinson's response was direct and went to the heart of who he was. "Mr. Rickey, are you looking for a Negro who is afraid to fight back?" asked Jackie. Rickey elaborated, explaining that whites would try to anger him and try to provoke black fans into a riot, all in hopes of ruining the experiment. He summarized in equally direct fashion: "Robinson, I'm looking for a ballplayer with guts enough not to fight back."[53]

Robinson pondered Rickey's words and the challenges they brought with it. His dreams matched those of every black athlete—to one day perform on the same field with white athletes, not as an exhibition, but as part of an integrated team whose players were chosen for their talent rather than their color.

Robinson wondered if he could manage his anger, and then realized that he had no choice. "Yet I knew that I must. I had to do it for so many reasons. For black youth, for my mother, for Rae [Rachel], for myself. I had already begun to feel I had to do it for Branch Rickey."[54] Robinson signed a contract for six hundred dollars a month and a thirty-five-hundred-dollar bonus to play for the Dodgers' minor league club in Montreal, Canada. Rickey asked Robinson to keep the deal secret until Rickey told him to spread the word.

"I'll Do My Very Best"

On October 23, 1945, the Dodger organization announced from their Montreal offices that they had signed a contract with Jackie Robinson to play baseball for them. Robinson told the press how delighted he was to help smash a racial barrier and how seriously he took the situation. "I realize how much it means to me, my race, and to baseball. I can only say I'll do my very best to come through in every manner."[55]

Black journalists recognized the significance of the Dodgers' move as well as its possible repercussions. White America would tend to judge all blacks based on Robinson's performance that first year. Should he fail, black Americans would fail with him. Edgar T. Rouzeau, a black columnist, wrote after the announcement,

In October 1945 Robinson smashes baseball's color barrier by signing contracts to play for the Montreal Royals.

The hopes and anxieties of the Negro race were placed squarely on the shoulders of Jack Roosevelt Robinson, the first of his clan to land a place in organized baseball. The announcement by the Brooklyn Dodgers . . . was received in Harlem [a black section of New York City] with a mixture of joy and trepidation.[56]

Before the 1946 regular season, Jackie traveled to Venezuela as part of a black all-star team. On this trip other players from the Negro League, including Roy Campanella, Cool Papa Bell, and first baseman Buck Leonard, helped Robinson hone his fielding, running, and batting skills, as they knew how significant his elevation to the Dodger system was. Gene Benson, Robinson's

An Important Moment

---■---

Blacks in the stands and elsewhere watched Jackie Robinson's first game as a major league player with apprehension. A dismal showing by Robinson, they knew, would hamper efforts to achieve complete integration, not just in baseball and other sports. Some even feared that integration in society as a whole would be slowed by a poor showing on Robinson's part. Sam Lacy of the Baltimore *Afro-American* wrote,

> Under these circumstances, it is easy to see why I felt a lump in my throat each time a ball was hit in his direction in those first few days; why I experienced a sort of emptiness in the bottom of my stomach whenever he took a swing in batting practice. I was constantly in fear of his muffing an easy roller under the stress of things. And I uttered a silent prayer of thanks as, with closed eyes, I heard the solid whack of Robinson's bat against the ball.

Arnold Rampersad, *Jackie Robinson: A Biography.* New York: Alfred A. Knopf, 1997, p. 147.

roommate in Venezuela, noticed that he already seemed to be feeling the burdens of representing black Americans. "Why did they pick me? Why did they pick me?"[57] Robinson was often heard muttering to no one in particular.

"I Was Scared"

Even as he was entering this crucial phase of his baseball career, Robinson was experiencing changes off the field too. He and Rachel married in Los Angeles on February 10, 1946. Both knew that they would be affected by his new job, and they engaged in a serious discussion of how to handle the coming months. Spring training, which always was held in Florida, was due to start in late February. This meant that he would soon face hostile Southern bigotry. They concluded that Jackie had to stick to his agreement with Branch Rickey and prevent his anger from bubbling over. "We had agreed that I had no right to lose my temper and jeopardize the chances of all the blacks who would follow me if I could help break down the barriers,"[58] Robinson wrote in his autobiography.

Thus mentally prepared, on February 28 the couple boarded an airplane for the first leg of a cross-country trip to Florida. Rachel, who had never been in the Jim Crow South, wondered if she was ready for the challenges that lay ahead and worried about safety.

Rachel noticed the first signs of segregation in the Deep South when the plane landed in New Orleans—separate water fountains for blacks and whites. Later, for reasons the Robinsons could never clearly determine, airline authorities told the couple that they had been bumped from the flight to Pensacola and would have to board a later flight. Eight hours later, after an irritating wait, they took off for Pensacola, Florida.

Upon arriving in New Orleans the Robinsons saw their first sign of the Deep South's segregation policies- seperate water fountains for blacks and whites.

When the plane landed in Florida, once again airline authorities informed Robinson that no room existed for them on the plane that was to take them to training camp. "I could see him seething," Rachel later recalled of her husband. "I thought he might hit somebody in his rage and then where would we be? I felt frightened now. I was scared, terrified."[59]

The two stifled their natural tendencies to argue and boarded a bus for the lengthy trip to Daytona Beach. They at first relaxed in reclining seats in the half-empty bus, but at one stop the driver harshly ordered them to the back row and its hard, wooden seats, despite the obvious availability of the more comfortable seats. Jackie quietly battled to maintain a semblance of calm, especially when he saw fear etched across Rachel's face. The couple walked past empty reclining seats to the black section in the rear, where they remained for the sixteen-hour trip.

During a 1946 game with the Brooklyn Dodgers, Robinson sits on the bench with Montreal Royals teammates, including Johnny Wright, another black player.

"I finally began to realize that where we were going with Mr. Rickey's plan, none of us had ever been before," Rachel stated later. "We were setting out on something we really didn't understand. And right in front of me, it was changing my life, changing who I was, or changing who I thought I was."[60]

On March 2, three days after leaving California, the Robinsons finally arrived in Daytona Beach, tired but now more cognizant of the challenges that lay ahead. Three black men, including Smith, met them at the station to help smooth their transition to life in the South and introduce them to other black residents.

A Rocky Start

Robinson's entrance into the once-exclusive major leagues was hardly encouraging. He and Rachel had to stay in a local black family's home instead of at the hotel with the white players. To avoid possible objection from white teammates to showering with a black man, a second home, closer to the ballpark, was made available where Robinson could shower and change into his uniform.

Manager Clay Hopper represented the emotions that many white players experienced. The Mississippi native told friends that he was happy his father was no longer alive, as he would probably kill his son for managing a black. He had begged Rickey to place Robinson on another team and claimed that if he had to manage the player he would have to sell his home in Mississippi and move his family out.

Rickey held firm. When Robinson arrived for the first day of spring training, more than one hundred white athletes halted their running and catching to stare as he walked across the ball field. As far as Robinson could tell, he did not have a single friend on the field.

Not surprisingly, resistance to integrated baseball in some of the Southern cities in which the Dodgers played games was extreme. The city of Jacksonville, Florida, padlocked the gates to the ball park because a city ordinance banned interracial competition. Savannah, Georgia, and Richmond, Virginia, did the same. In one game at Sanford, Florida, the town's chief of police halted the game in the third inning and ordered Hopper to remove Robinson from the lineup.

"Thanks, George"

On April 18 Robinson made his regular season debut in a game against the Jersey City Giants at Jersey City, New Jersey. After grounding out to the shortstop in the first inning, Robinson powered a ball over the fence for a home run in the third. As he rounded third and headed for home, Robinson wondered if anyone would congratulate him for the feat or if they would continue the game as if nothing happened. He did not have to wait long as George Shuba, the next batter, waited by home plate with his hand extended to offer congratulations. When newspapers ran photos of the handshake the next day, Robinson walked over to Shuba. "Thanks, George,"[61] he said of the welcome gesture.

Royals teammate George Shuba congratulates Robinson as he crosses home plate after a home run on opening day in 1946.

Even better was the affection of the crowd, which appreciated his combination of power, hitting, and speed. By game's end they were cheering wildly for Robinson. "I knew what it was that day to hear the ear-shattering roar of the crowd and know it was for me," wrote Robinson. "I began to really believe one of Mr. Rickey's predictions. Color didn't matter to fans if the black man was a winner."[62]

The elation only lasted until the next series of games, scheduled for Baltimore, Maryland, where fans directed a torrent of verbal abuse at Robinson. Two men sitting behind Rachel yelled profanities at the player all game long, including calling Robinson a "nigger son of a bitch."[63] Rachel sat quietly in the stands, stoically bearing this horrible treatment of her husband, knowing that there was nothing to gain by speaking out.

"A Heavy Burden of Responsibility"

After the first two series, the team headed to Montreal for the opening series of games at home. Montreal's obvious affection for the team, and for Robinson in particular, touched Jackie and Rachel. The two were astounded at how quickly and willingly white residents chatted with them and how easy it was to rent an apartment in a largely white neighborhood. Montreal residents accepted them as if they had always lived in the Canadian city, cheered the team during games, and appeared not to notice any difference in skin color.

"I owe more to Canadians than they'll ever know," recalled Robinson. "In my baseball career they were the first to make me feel my natural self." He warmly recalled the French-speaking fan who loved to bellow in fractured English throughout the game, "Jackie, 'e's my boy!"[64]

Once away from Montreal's sanctuary and back in the United States, however, Robinson faced more bigotry. Members of the Syracuse, New York, team tossed a black cat onto the field and yelled, "Hey, Jackie, there's your cousin."[65] Insults greeted him almost every time he stepped on the field.

Besides Rachel's emotional support, what kept Robinson going was the conviction that by persevering he would help blacks attain equality in other walks of life. Robinson noticed that as the season went by, larger numbers of black fans appeared in the stands, even in Southern cities where seating was segregated. He believed that he held their hopes and dreams in his hands, a responsibility that sometimes weighed on him.

> Their presence, their cheers, their pride, all came through to me and I knew they were counting on me to make it. It put a heavy burden of responsibility on me, but it was a glorious challenge. On the good days the cries of approval made me feel ten feet tall, but my mistakes, no matter how small, plunged me into deep depression.[66]

Robinson felt even more a sense of responsibility when Rachel informed him in June that she was expecting their first child. An ecstatic Robinson almost cried for joy at the news, and promised his wife that they would enjoy a happy life with their child.

"You're a Great Ballplayer"

That minor league season ended on a high for Robinson and the Montreal Royals as they met the Louisville Colonels for the championship. Louisville fans verbally harassed Robinson as he registered only one hit as his team lost two of the first three games, but conditions swiftly changed when the team returned to Montreal. Upset that their player had been so harshly treated by the Louisville fans, Montreal supporters packed the stadium to cheer on their heroes and to give a taste of similar medicine to the opponents. Every time a Louisville player stepped to the plate, Montreal fans booed lustily, and whenever a Montreal player batted, cheers rocked the stadium. Fueled by the support, Robinson went on a hitting spree, and the Royals took the next three games to capture the championship.

Crazed fans mobbed the players after the final out. "They grabbed me, they slapped my back. They hugged me. Women kissed me. Kids grinned and crowded around me,"[67] Robinson wrote later. People hoisted players to their shoulders and marched around the stadium in triumph, and even chased after them as they exited the park. At one point, Robinson had to rush down a street to avoid five hundred delirious fans. After a three-block sprint, he was finally saved by teammates who pulled up in a car. A sportswriter, cognizant of racial relations in the United States and aware that during the decades since the end of slavery

Demise of Negro League Baseball

———————————————◼———————————————

One of the ironic consequences of Robinson's entry into major league baseball was that as more black athletes followed, fewer would remain to play in the Negro League. Club owners had long profited from black fans attending games involving black athletes, but with the top players soon defecting to the major leagues, black baseball had less and less talented play to offer the fans. Attendance plummeted, clubs went bankrupt, and the league went out of existence.

Some black baseball clubs tried to slow the hemorrhaging of talent. The Kansas City Monarchs even threatened to sue the Brooklyn Dodgers for stealing Jackie Robinson, but seeing that public sentiment favored the player, decided to let him go without a fight.

numerous blacks had been killed by rampaging mobs, wrote, "It was probably the only day in history that a black man ran from a white mob with love instead of lynching on its mind."[68]

Robinson's quality play before and during the final series won over many of his detractors. In a telling transformation, Hopper, the Royals' manager and one of Robinson's bitterest critics, walked over to Robinson, shook his hand, and said, "You're a great ballplayer and a fine gentleman. It's been wonderful having you on the team." The manager from Mississippi later told reporters that Robinson had earned his respect and that he was "a player who must go to the majors."[69]

Hopper had plenty of company in that opinion. Branch Rickey had maintained a close watch on Robinson all year. Although Rickey chose not to say so directly to Robinson, the time had come to bring him into the major leagues.

Chapter Five

"Well, You Made It"

As spring training of 1947 approached, Robinson's life was changing in many ways. For the first time he was faced with the responsibilities of parenthood, because on November 18, 1946, Jack Roosevelt Robinson Jr. had been born. Secondly, he faced the possibility that 1947 would be the year he made it to the major leagues.

Number 42

Branch Rickey let Robinson know how important this spring training was before it started. In an effort to showcase Robinson's talents, Rickey had scheduled a number of exhibition games pitting the Royals against their parent club, the Brooklyn Dodgers. Robinson fulfilled Rickey's wishes by amassing a .625 batting average and stealing seven bases in seven games against the Dodgers. Most of the Dodgers were impressed with his exploits, but a small group of players circulated a petition stating that they would not play if the Dodgers promoted Robinson to the big league team.

The rebellion was short-lived, for one of the team's leaders, shortstop Pee Wee Reese, stunned the protesters by declining to sign. They had expected the native Kentuckian, who had grown up under segregation, to support their effort, but Reese was not to be swayed. He had a family to support and feared losing money should he join the boycott. More than that, Reese believed in treating people with respect, regardless of race. "I can't sign this thing,"[70] he told his disgruntled teammates. Without Reese's support, the petition drive floundered.

On April 9, 1947, the Dodgers announced that they were bringing Jackie Robinson to the parent club from Montreal. Hopper told Robinson, "I knew we couldn't keep you long. I sure wanted to, but this is your big chance. Now go out there and make good."[71]

Robinson wondered what reception awaited him when he walked into the Dodger clubhouse. Pitcher Carl Erskine later

In his first at-bat as a full-fledged Brooklyn Dodger, Robinson grounds out to third at Ebbets Field in April 1947.

Pee Wee Reese

Born July 23, 1918, in Ekron, Kentucky, Harold Henry "Pee Wee" Reese joined the major leagues in April 1940. His sound play and decency as an individual soon made him a team favorite, and he later captained some of the most successful Dodger teams in history.

Called Pee Wee because of his skill in playing marbles—a pee wee is a type of marble—Reese helped smooth Jackie Robinson's transition into the major leagues. He welcomed the newcomer by showing opponents and fans alike that Robinson was his teammate and friend, regardless of color. When Reese was inducted into baseball's Hall of Fame in 1984, his plaque's inscription cited him not only for his stellar play but for his role in helping Jackie Robinson break the color barrier.

When Reese died in August 1999, friends praised him for his courageous stand against bigotry. One writer claimed that the incident in which Reese placed his arm about Robinson's shoulder to counter blistering verbal abuse was one of baseball's finest moments.

Friends and teammates Jackie Robinson and Pee Wee Reese smile after Game 1 of the 1952 World Series.

wrote of a mixed reaction, "with few players adamantly against Jackie, even fewer adamantly for him, and the majority in a neutral position."[72] Most of his teammates decided to let events demonstrate how skilled Robinson really was.

On April 15, in Brooklyn's packed Ebbets Field, Robinson played in his first major league game. Wearing the number "42" on his uniform, he walked to the plate for his initial at-bat with the importance of the moment blocking out his focus. In the stands, a proud but apprehensive Rachel watched her husband, and "the meaning of the moment for me seemed to transcend the winning of a ballgame. The possibility of social change seemed more concrete, and the need for it seemed more imperative."[73]

It hardly mattered that Robinson failed to register a base hit in four trips to the plate against the Boston Braves. The Dodgers won, 5-3, and Robinson had opened the major leagues for other African Americans.

"What Was I Doing Here?"

The import of smashing baseball's color barrier distracted Robinson in the early part of the season. He failed to register a single hit in his first five games. Events over which Robinson had little control affected his play. For example, as expected, he was subject to a torrent of abuse from fans and opposing players. Rachel wrote later that "every stadium that year was a battleground." For Robinson, the situation was made even more difficult by his promise to Rickey that he would not react. "All of his instincts cried out for release to retaliate,"[74] explained Rachel. Having to quietly go about his business and block out the negative atmosphere went against all of Robinson's instincts.

Maintaining an even keel was no easier for Rachel, who endured hearing a torrent of hate directed at Robinson. Whenever fans called her husband "nigger" or shouted for him to go back to the jungle, Rachel reacted by sitting up as straight as possible, asserting her dignity by refusing to cower or lash out.

An early series against the Philadelphia Phillies set the tone. Led by manager Ben Chapman, the Phillies let loose with a non-stop barrage of racial slurs. "Hey, nigger, why don't you go back to the cotton field where you belong?" shouted one player, while another bellowed, "They're waiting for you in the jungles, black

Tension is evident in this photo of Robinson and Phillies' manager Ben Chapman in 1947, after Chapman encouraged his team to harass Robinson.

boy!" and a third yelled, "We don't want you here, nigger!"[75] These remarks stunned Robinson, who did not expect such a harsh reaction in a Northern city.

Robinson was deeply conflicted as he decided whether to react. "What was I doing here turning the other cheek as though I weren't a man?" He had rarely backed down, even in the army. Was he to allow these hateful comments to pass? "Then, I thought of Mr. Rickey—how his family and friends had begged him not to fight for me and my people."[76]

By the third day of the series some of Robinson's teammates came to his aid by responding to the Phillies. Eddie Stanky shouted, "Listen, you yellow-bellied cowards, why don't you yell at somebody who can answer back?" The support from his white teammates calmed Robinson, who later wrote "It was then that I began to feel better."[77]

In the next series, against the St. Louis Cardinals, the bigotry took a more organized form. Cardinals players planned to walk off the field before the team's first game against the Dodgers on May 9. This time the major league baseball commissioner, Ford Frick stepped in, threatening to suspend anyone who participated. He promised to do so, in his words, "even if it wrecks the National League for five years. This is the United States of America, and one citizen has as much right to play as another."[78]

Players spiked Robinson on the shins—that is, sliding into base with their cleats high, or they made not-so-subtle threats by pointing baseball bats at him while making sounds mimicking gunfire. In Philadelphia the Benjamin Franklin Hotel, named after one of the signers of the Declaration of Independence, refused to allow Robinson to stay with the team. He and Rachel gathered their suitcases and headed to a nearby YMCA.

Rachel proved to be a stalwart supporter during this and subsequent turbulent moments in Robinson's life. Away from the park they sought refuge in simple things, like long bus rides together about New York and laughter at each other's jokes. They held to the mutual conviction that conditions would slowly improve as the season progressed, and that next year would be even better.

"You're Doing Fine"

Still, the Robinsons could never completely escape the bitterness of race hatred even when at home. Hate mail arrived almost every day, some threatening to kill Robinson or Rachel. "We have already got rid of several like you," warned the writer of one letter. "One was found in the river just recently." A note signed by "The Travelers" stated, "We are going to kill you if you attempt to enter a ball game at Crosley Field [Cincinnati]."[79] Robinson handed over most of the threatening letters to the Dodgers, who forwarded them to the local authorities.

In one pregame warm-up, Robinson showed Pee Wee Reese a threat he had received. In it, the writer warned Robinson that if he played in that game, he would be shot. Reese read the letter, then joked, "Jack. Don't stand so close to me today. Move away, will ya?"[80] His remark produced laughter and lightened the grim situation.

As the season progressed, a few encouraging letters appeared along with the hate mail. One came from a southerner:

> Jackie: I am a white man, who like many thousands of other white people, feel that in our American way of life we should not tolerate race prejudice and that a person will be judged on his merits. I send you congratulations and believe you will be a credit to baseball, just as Joe Louis has been to boxing.[81]

Supportive remarks like that came only in a trickle, but they helped counter the bitter reactions to his presence in the game.

Rickey told Robinson that when his teammates had begun to openly support him, that would constitute a great stride toward normalcy. Once again, Pee Wee Reese provided that. During a series in Boston, opposing players and fans taunted Robinson bitterly, and even berated Reese for playing with a black. Reese quietly walked over to Robinson, put one arm around his shoulder, and chatted in an openly friendly manner with his teammate, as if saying to the detractors that their words meant nothing. "I don't even remember what he said," Jackie later wrote. "It was the gesture of comradeship and support that counted."[82]

On May 17 Robinson heard the first encouraging words from an opposing player. Hank Greenberg of the Pittsburgh Pirates, the first Jewish player in the Major Leagues, stood at first base after a walk and said to Robinson, "Listen, don't pay any attention to these guys who are trying to make it hard for you. Stick in there. You're doing fine. The next time you come to Pittsburgh, I hope you and I can get together for a talk. There are a few things I've learned down through the years that might help you and make it easier."[83]

Rookie of the Year

Robinson decided the best way to counter racism was to prove that he belonged in the major leagues. He thought that once the fans and his opponents realized that he could play at the level of major leaguers, most would accept his presence. Finally, on May 10 he halted his slump at the plate with a double, a single, and two runs scored. His performance led Sukeforth to tell Jackie that he was ready to explode.

He continued the hot streak for the next few weeks, gaining his teammates' praise and their willingness to treat him as any

Humor and a Death Threat

◼

That Robinson received death threats was nothing unusual, but one in Cincinnati stood out for the humor that marked it. Pitcher Carl Erskine recalled that the Dodgers' manager assembled the entire team and read the threat to the hushed crowd. As Erskine recalled, "The clubhouse was real quiet as he read these nasty things about how Jackie was going to have his head blown off if he walked on the field. You could feel the tension in the room."

Gene Hermanski instantly dissolved the dire atmosphere in a few words. The player remarked, tongue in cheek, "If we all go out on the field wearing number 42 on our uniforms, they wouldn't know which one of us to shoot."

The obviously facetious comment made everyone laugh, broke the tension, and enabled the team to head to the diamond in a more positive frame of mind.

Maury Allen, *Jackie Robinson: A Life Remembered.* New York: Franklin Watts, 1987, p. 165.

Teammates Gene Hermanski (left), Robinson, and Gil Hodges show the order of a killer triple play in a 1949 game.

Robinson's outstanding base stealing gets him onto second base in a 1947 World Series game at Yankee Stadium.

other player. They asked him to play cards in the clubhouse and included him in the usual teasing and banter that they used to fill the hours before games. "I didn't feel like a sideshow freak any more. Better still, I was beginning to feel that I was really an important part of the team." One time, after he flubbed a routine play and was charged with an error, the friendly jibes from team-mates were music to his ears. "I was laughing with joy because I knew now that I was one of Brooklyn's beloved Bums."[84]

Robinson noticed that even the fans had begun to notice his on-field exploits. During one June game against Pittsburgh, even the opposing fans cheered lustily when Robinson stole home to put the Dodgers ahead 3-2. Spectators loved watching Robinson take wide turns on singles, as if daring the outfielder to throw the ball behind him to first base in an attempt to pick him off. Few did, as they knew the speedy Robinson would only charge toward second and beat the relay.

By late August Robinson had become a key member of the team. When Enos Slaughter of the St. Louis Cardinals spiked Robinson's leg, teammates rushed onto the field in a brawl that made the point that their fellow player was to be respected. For the remainder of the season, the Dodgers competed with a newfound dedication.

A crucial August swing against four close rivals sealed the pennant for the Dodgers. Robinson led the way by batting .408 in the games, with three home runs and five stolen bases. His performance during this key period had other managers praising Robinson as the most improved player in the league.

The Dodgers clinched the pennant on the road. When they returned to Brooklyn, an ecstatic mob welcomed them at the train station, then pursued Robinson and the other players as they headed to catch taxicabs. One group cornered Robinson in a phone booth, where he remained until police could extricate him from the crowd of cheering fans.

The *Sporting News* honored Robinson by naming him as the Rookie of the Year, not because he had broken the color barrier, but for what he had accomplished on the field. He finished nineteenth

Robinson accepts the J. Louis Comiskey award from the Baseball Writers Association in 1947, one of many honors and awards he received during his career.

in the league with a .296 batting average (which included 31 doubles, 12 home runs, and 48 runs batted in) he led the league with 29 stolen bases and placed second in total runs scored with 125. A few days before the end of the season, the Dodgers held a "Jackie Robinson Day" at Ebbets Field and presented their young player with a new car, a television set, and other gifts.

"A Member of a Solid Team"

Robinson carried over his exploits to postseason play, where he became the first black ballplayer to participate in a World Series. Standing in the middle of historic Yankee Stadium, bedecked in colorful banners and packed with fans that included former president Herbert Hoover, Robinson experienced unexpected emotions that September day. He later stated that the first season had offered both bitterness and joy, "but it wasn't until I was standing before the World Series crowd in Yankee Stadium, watching the flag flutter upward in center field and hearing the wonderful sounds of our national anthem, that I felt able to say to myself, for the first time, 'Well, you made it.'"[85]

For the first time, television provided national coverage of the World Series. While Robinson's play was overshadowed by that of the great Joe DiMaggio and other Yankee stars, who took the series in seven games from the Dodgers, it was Robinson who grabbed the nation's attention. "The television pictures for that Series were in black-and-white," stated sportswriter Red Barber.

> For the first time—and forever after—the players were also black-and-white. Jackie Robinson captured all attention when he got on base. People who hadn't seen Jackie dance off first, draw a throw, dart back . . . dance off again, worry the pitcher, draw a throw, dart back . . . dance off, and GO . . . and make it safely at second! . . . could hardly believe the testimony of their startled eyes.[86]

After the final game in the series, Barber, who also routinely covered the Dodgers as the play-by-play radio announcer, walked around the clubhouse shaking hands with the players. He noticed that despite having just lost the series to the Yankees, many of the Dodgers shook hands with Robinson and told him what a fine ballplayer he was.

Robinson and Robeson

In July 1949 Robinson was asked to testify before the United States House Un-American Activities Committee. The committee was looking into remarks by black singer Paul Robeson that blacks would not fight for the United States should the Cold War turn into actual military conflict.

Robinson disagreed with Robeson, but was unsure what to do. If he declined the invitation, he could be seen as disrespectful of the committee. If he testified and disagreed with Robeson, it would pit him against Robeson, a popular entertainer. At the same time, Robinson feared that Robeson's comment harmed the image of blacks in the eyes of the nation and made them appear to be unpatriotic. He felt that Robeson did not speak for all blacks, so he decided to testify.

In his statement before the committee, Robinson agreed with Robeson that much prejudice existed in the country, but he said that he believed Robeson was incorrect in his assessment of African Americans' loyalty. He told the committee he cherished his nation and he believed that most African Americans felt the same way. He added, however, that like Robeson, he would continue to battle racism wherever he saw it.

Jackie Robinson testifies on black patriotism before the House Un-American Activities Committee in Washington, D.C., in 1949.

During Game 6 of the 1947 World Series, Robinson slides into second base breaking up a double play as Yankees shortstop Phil Rizzuto leaps over him.

Jackie felt he had accomplished what he and Rickey had hoped. "I had started the season as a lonely man, often feeling like a black Don Quixote tilting at a lot of windmills. I ended it feeling like a member of a solid team."[87]

The effect of Robinson's success was quickly visible in major league baseball. Already, other blacks had been signed to play in the major leagues. For example, the Cleveland Indians signed outfielder Larry Doby in July, eleven weeks after Jackie first stepped onto the field. One month later, Henry Thompson and Willard Brown signed major league contracts. In all, sixteen black ballplayers competed in either the minor or the major leagues in 1947.

Rachel Robinson noticed that as the season unfolded, white fans increasingly cheered Jackie's efforts, leading her to think that true progress in racial relations might be made. Mainly, though, Jackie and Rachel realized what the year meant to fellow blacks and were proud they could contribute in their own way. "On the personal side," Rachel wrote, "Jack and I began to realize how important we were to black America, and how much we symbolized its hunger for opportunity and its determination to make dreams long deferred possible."[88]

He had won the first round. The question remained whether that victory could be carried over to following years and to society at large.

Chapter Six

"We Wanted to Be Part of Him"

In 1947 Robinson had successfully opened the major leagues to black athletes. However, his contributions to baseball did not end there. He amassed a brilliant record on the field and off over the next ten years. Afterward, he contributed significantly to society in other ways.

"Attaboy, Jackie"

The next year started in rough fashion. In the off-season Robinson had been in Hollywood, California, assisting in the production of a film, *The Jackie Robinson Story*. When he returned for spring training in 1948, Robinson sported twenty-five extra pounds of weight. Jackie later admitted that he did not reach his top shape until mid-season. Despite the additional poundage, Jackie eventually compiled impressive numbers, again batting close to .300 and leading the league in fielding for second basemen, the position to which he had been shifted from first base.

Robinson approached the 1949 season with relish. For two years he had kept his word to Rickey that he would not respond to racial slurs from players, but the proud player no longer had to stifle his urge to speak back. Rickey gave him the discretion to react to racist remarks.

He arrived at camp in superb condition and remarked to a sportswriter that they would see a different Jackie Robinson. The first time he encountered Chapman, the Philadelphia Phillies manager who had orchestrated such horrendous verbal abuse toward Robinson in 1947, he walked toward him and said, "Look, Chapman, you son of a bitch. You got on me for two years and I couldn't say a word. Now you open your mouth to me one more time during this game, I'm gonna catch you and I'm gonna kick the . . . out of you."[89] Robinson had no more problems with Chapman after that.

Robinson compiled a most impressive season indeed in 1949, sparking the team to another World Series while leading the National League in batting with a .342 average. Though they again lost to the Yankees, Robinson was named the league's Most Valuable

Jackie Robinson, shown here with actress Louise Beavers, played himself in *The Jackie Robinson Story*.

Player and given a contract for 1950 worth a hefty thirty-five thousand dollars, quite heady for its day.

As happy as he was with his on-field numbers, Robinson was prouder of the rapport he seemed to have with young people. Not trapped in the quagmire of bigotry as so many adults were, young boys and girls cheered lustily for their heroes, white and black. "They just wanted me to be good, to deliver, to win," he wrote. "The inspiration of their innocence is amazing. I don't think I'll ever forget the small, shrill voice of a tiny white kid who, in the midst of a racially tense atmosphere during an early game in a Dixie [Southern] town, cried out, 'Attaboy, Jackie.' It broke the tension and it made me feel I had to succeed."[90]

Pitcher Preacher Roe compared him to "an alley fighter, he wanted to win so bad. He wanted to win at everything: baseball,

In the 1955 World Series, Robinson safely steals home despite attempts by Yankee catcher Yogi Berra to tag him out.

cards, shooting pool, everything."[91] Another Dodgers pitcher, Don Newcombe, explained that if he lost his focus on the mound, Jackie would trot over from second base and call him every name in the book. Newcombe would get angry at Robinson, then take it out on the hitters.

Robinson and the Dodgers amassed an amazing string of seasons from 1949–1956. They captured five pennants, tied for one, and lost another on the season's final day. In 1955 fueled by a Robinson theft of home in the first game, they brought home to Brooklyn a World Series championship. Robinson batted over .300 in six of the eight seasons, only falling below the magical mark in 1955, when hamstring injuries and other nagging problems dating back to college sports hampered the star, and in 1956, his final season. Robinson went out in grand style as his last hit in the major leagues came in the sixth game of the 1956 World Series when he slugged in the game-winning run.

"I'm Getting There *Today*"

Robinson's contribution to baseball went well beyond his on-field performance. True to his word, Robinson battled segregation wherever he encountered it. In his final years as a Dodger he often drew the wrath of sportswriters and baseball executives, who argued that he was more concerned with social issues than with playing baseball. Robinson spoke to civic groups, appeared on radio and television, and assisted organizations such as the NAACP in their efforts to gain equality for African Americans.

Robinson approached his work on behalf of equality with the same energy as when he ran the base paths. Most illustrative was Robinson's determination to end the practice in St. Louis of segregated accommodations when the team played. While the white players enjoyed air-conditioned rooms at a luxurious hotel, the black players had been relegated to second-class accommodations elsewhere in the town. Jackie intended to halt that practice.

When the team bus pulled up to the Chase Hotel, Roy Campanella and the other blacks on the Dodgers stepped off and headed toward cabs that would whisk them to their hotel. Jackie refused to budge from the bus.

"Hey. Come with us, Jack," shouted Campanella.

"No. I'm going to the Chase."

Robinson, shown here hitting the ball in the World Series of 1955, was known as much for battling segregation as he was for his superb ball playing.

"Oh, man. Come on," stated a concerned Campanella. "We'll all get in the Chase eventually."

"I know," replied Robinson. "But I'm getting there *today*."[92] Robinson had taken enough abuse throughout the years and was not willing to wait for society to alter things on its own. His firm stance forced hotel management to alter their segregated arrangements and accept the entire team.

Robinson and Campanella often argued over how aggressively integration should be pursued. Campanella was pleased simply to be in the major leagues and did not want to make waves, while Robinson insisted that more had to be done as quickly as possible. "Just because we are here, it doesn't mean the problem is solved,"[93] he reminded his teammate.

Robinson understood that the breaking of baseball's color barrier was only a beginning. Years later he recalled with bitterness how the team's white trainers, whose job was to rub down the players after a game, refused to touch him. Instead, Robinson was forced to wait until he arrived home, where Rachel would massage his sore muscles.

Robinson's teammates sympathized with how the refusal of some fans to accept him rankled Robinson. "We would take the field," recalled teammate and Hall of Fame pitcher Don Drysdale of the 1956 season, "and there would always be some loudmouth there to scream at him from behind a dozen other fans. It was a long time after he had broken in, he was a great star, and he still had to take that abuse. What could he do, run in the stands and fight all of them who called him a name?"[94]

Robinson persisted because, he said, surrounded by the demons of bigotry, bright signs appeared. He noticed that as the years passed, more white fans cheered for black players, even during the spring training games that were held in the South. By the time he retired in 1956, more than fifty black ballplayers would be competing in the majors, with another one hundred in the minor leagues.

A Hall of Famer

Even as Robinson was seeing positive outcomes for his efforts, the physical demands of baseball were taking their toll. He had to sit out more games than usual, and those flashes of speed on the base paths occurred less often. Robinson was ready to consider retiring from baseball. Moreover, his family was growing, and his frequent absences on road trips were keenly felt. Daughter Sharon had been born on January 13, 1950, followed by son David on May 14, 1952. He and Rachel purchased a beautiful home along a small lake in Stamford, Connecticut, a suburban town offering excellent schools and pleasant neighborhoods.

His baseball capabilities declined. Arthritic knees, the result of many years of hard smashes in football, basketball, and baseball, hampered his base running. Robinson sat on the bench more and more during the 1956 season.

In mid-December 1956 William Black, the owner of Chock Full o' Nuts Coffee, quietly offered Jackie forty thousand dollars to be vice president in charge of personnel for his company. And because 70 percent of the company's employees were black, Robinson would be in a position to directly help other African

The Robinson family relaxes at their Stamford, Connecticut, home in 1966.

Americans. At the same time, *Look* magazine dangled fifty thousand dollars if Robinson agreed to announce his retirement, whenever it occurred, in an exclusive interview.

In December 1956, at the age of thirty-seven, Robinson said farewell to major league baseball. With sports consuming his time since his childhood days, he looked to a future where other endeavors would occupy his time. Robinson continued to labor on behalf of racial equality. He spoke at inner-city schools and for the NAACP, urging students to work hard and set goals. He hosted a radio show and wrote a newspaper column, both of which served as forums to express his ideas on how African Americans could attain a better life. In 1956 he crossed the nation on behalf of the NAACP's Freedom Fund, raising money for various civil rights projects, and he started the Freedom Bank to assist blacks in establishing businesses and developing economic power.

"It's incomprehensible to estimate the number of lives Jackie saved through his public speaking engagements at inner-city schools," pitcher and teammate Carl Erskine said of Jackie's work with young people. He added that because of Jackie's baseball clinics and appearances, "kids played baseball and stayed off the streets."[95]

Awards for his civil rights work and his record-setting performance in baseball came in one after another. On December 8, 1956, he received the NAACP's Spingarn Medal, a prestigious honor bestowed on only forty-one people before Robinson, including the famous African American inventor, George Washington Carver.

Dozens of Boy Scouts and Cub Scouts crowd around Jackie Robinson to shake his hand In 1953.

The award he most coveted, entry into baseball's Hall of Fame, followed six years later when he was inducted at Cooperstown, New York, on July 23, 1962. Speaking to a crowd of five thousand Jackie gave credit to the individuals who he said were most responsible for this happy moment. "I feel quite inadequate to this honor. It is something that could never have happened without three people—Branch Rickey, who was as a father to me, my wife and my mother. They are all here today, making the honor complete."[96]

The NAACP later held a dinner to honor Robinson. Remarks from Martin Luther King Jr. praised the athlete for bringing hope to future generations of youngsters regardless of race.

More and more, civil rights leaders turned to the baseball star to aid their cause. In June 1963, with the civil rights movement gaining momentum, Robinson met with King to discuss ways the baseball star could help. When King stated that money was needed to free arrested civil rights marchers, Jackie and Rachel hosted the Afternoon of Jazz at their home. Legendary singers and musicians such as Ella Fitzgerald and Duke Ellington performed at the charity event, which would continue to be held each June in Connecticut even into the next century.

Hard Times

Robinson believed that the best way of achieving equality was for blacks to work within the system, to cooperate with those in power in hopes of gaining equality. Those civil rights groups and leaders who employed more radical methods, such as Malcolm X and the Black Panthers, spurned his stance. Some leaders grew frustrated and began advocating violence.

One move by Robinson, during the 1960 presidential campaign, even alienated other moderates within the civil rights movement. He met privately with both major candidates—conservative Republican candidate Richard Nixon and his liberal Democratic opponent, John F. Kennedy—and came away more impressed with the Republican. He endorsed Nixon and campaigned on his behalf at a time when every other major black leader supported Kennedy.

Criticism by black activists took its toll and added to his other problems. He had struggled for several years with diabetes and

At a political rally in 1960, Richard Nixon shakes hands with Robinson, who surprised everyone with his endorsement of Nixon during the presidential campaign.

an accompanying loss of sight. He had also gained weight and become cynical over future prospects for blacks. Strain led to two mild heart attacks later in the decade. He even distanced himself from baseball, appearing at only a handful of old-timers' games.

Personal tragedy then struck. On May 21, 1968, the seventy-eight-year-old Mallie Robinson collapsed as she walked up the driveway to her Pepper Street home. A grief-stricken Robinson took the first plane to California, but Mallie succumbed before he reached her bedside. The loss of one of the most influential persons in his life was difficult for Robinson. For years she had been the glue that held the family together, and now she was gone.

Difficulties with his son, Jackie Jr., exacerbated the situation. The younger Robinson had enlisted in the military and had gone to Vietnam in 1965. There, he was injured in an explosion that killed two soldiers standing next to him. When Jackie Jr. returned home in 1967, he was suffering from a serious addiction to heroin and other drugs. The young man's troubles grew even worse after a 1968 arrest for drug and weapons possession led to his incarceration for three years in the Daytop Rehabilitation Program in Seymour, Connecticut. The elder Robinson ruefully noted his lack of success with his own son: "I guess I had more of an effect on other people's kids than I had on my own."[97]

The three years of confinement transformed Jackie Jr., who remained at the center as a drug counselor to others in trouble. When the elder Robinson held a fund-raising benefit for the center, father and son tightly embraced, relishing the fact that both had grown close. Rachel watched from feet away and later said, "Jack's eyes filled with tears—he had his son back."[98]

That happiness ended tragically when, in June 1971, Jackie Jr. was killed in an automobile accident. The death of his son crushed Robinson. "You don't know what it's like to lose a son [to drug addiction], find him, and lose him again,"[99] he sadly wrote.

"I Love You"

His sorrow over his son's death combined with other health problems to age Robinson. On April 6, 1972, he attended the funeral of former teammate Gil Hodges, and Pee Wee Reese was stunned at how poorly his friend looked. "Jack just looked older than I had remembered him. He seemed to have trouble walking, and he absolutely couldn't see. It was so sad. You just forget how the years go on, and all of a sudden we are all grandfathers. Jackie just seemed to get older faster than the rest of us. It had to be what he went through. I don't think Jack ever stopped carrying that burden. I'm no doctor but I'm sure it cut his life short. Jackie Robinson never could stop fighting."[100]

In June 1972 Robinson flew to Los Angeles, where the Dodgers had relocated, to be honored by the team in a ceremony at which his number was to be retired—an honor accorded only a select few players in any sport. From that date on, no Dodger would ever wear 42 on his uniform. Major League baseball later retired Jackie's number from the entire league—no one would ever again don Jackie's number in a professional baseball game.

Curt Flood

In 1969 baseball player Curt Flood made history in the sport when he refused to report to his new team after being traded from the St. Louis Cardinals to the Philadelphia Phillies. He claimed that baseball denied his right as an individual to select the team for whom he wanted to play, and he sued over baseball's rule that gave owners great freedom in sending a player from one team to another without the player's permission.

The case eventually went to superior court in New York for a decision. As Flood sat in the courtroom with his lawyers, he suddenly saw Jackie Robinson enter the room.

As Flood remembered, "I was in the courtroom that day, and Jackie Robinson walked in, and I got a lump in my throat." Flood was moved because he had not contacted Robinson. The man appeared on his own to testify on Flood's behalf.

"All I know is that I will never forget that day Jackie came to that courtroom, and I will always owe a debt to his memory. He didn't have to do that. Nobody called him to do it. He just showed up, just volunteered his story because he wanted to do it, because he simply thought it was right."

Because of Flood's courageous stand, in part aided by Robinson's surprise courtroom appearance, major league baseball players now enjoy greater freedom in deciding what team to join.

Maury Allen, *Jackie Robinson: A Life Remembered.* New York: Franklin Watts, 1987, pp. 230–31.

Robinson's final public appearance occurred on October 15, 1972, at Game 2 of the World Series, when baseball marked the occasion to honor the twenty-fifth anniversary of his entry into the major leagues in 1947. Robinson rapidly declined after the World Series. Failing eyesight forced him to rely on a chauffeur to drive him around, and the diabetes and extra weight slowed him further.

In late October 1972, Jackie and Rachel were watching a football game on television when he told her that he had just experienced a bright flash in one eye. Such a development was ominous, since it often is a sign that a blood vessel in the eye has ruptured. Fearing the onset of complete blindness, they arranged an appointment to see his physician the next morning. "The devastating prognosis of blindness lingered in the air that night as we fell asleep in a tight embrace," wrote Rachel.

As Rachel prepared breakfast the next morning, Jackie rushed down the hallway from his bedroom, put his arms around his wife, said, "I love you," and collapsed. An ambulance raced him from his home, but Robinson died before reaching the hospital. "My dearest Jack, my giant, had been struck down, striving to live and loving to the very end,"[101] said Rachel of her husband's death on October 24. Robinson was only fifty-three years old.

Three days later twenty-five hundred people, including sports celebrities and civil rights leaders, gathered at Riverside Church in New York City. His longtime friend, Pee Wee Reese, who had done so much to help Jackie endure the pressure of his early years with the Dodgers, served as a pallbearer. In his eulogy the Reverend

Friends and teammates, including pallbearers Pee Wee Reese and Don Newcombe, say a final good-bye to Jackie Robinson on October 27, 1972.

Jesse Jackson, who was a rising figure in the civil rights movement, praised Robinson's work in shattering stereotypes and giving hope to so many youngsters. Jackson said the ballplayer's struggle directly led to major advances in civil rights, such as the 1954 Supreme Court case outlawing segregated schools. A long procession then transported Robinson's body to Cypress Hills Cemetery in Brooklyn, the city of his baseball exploits.

"I Owe Everything to Jackie Robinson"

Robinson's impact on baseball is undeniable, yet in the decades since his death many people have begun to forget his contributions. If it were up to Robinson's teammates, this would change. Don Newcombe said, "I owe everything I have, everything I have made in my life through baseball, to Jackie Robinson. I want young people, especially young black people, to know the history, to know the battles he fought, the racism, the turmoil he went through."[102]

Jackie's roommate on that long-ago trip to Venezuela, Gene Benson, talked to Robinson about what his being in the majors would mean for black athletes. Benson saw at the time the toll the pressure was taking on the young man. "He was high-strung, so much so that he paid with his life to go through what he had to. It caused him an early death because he just blew up inside. But Jackie was a man who would do anything to help one of his own. That was his secret, you understand? He went out and gave his life for black athletes."[103]

Before his death in 1968, the prominent civil rights leader Martin Luther King Jr. spoke of Jackie Robinson's importance to his own life. "You will never know how easy it was for me because of Jackie Robinson,"[104] he said of the athlete who paved the way for his civil rights movement. Rosa Parks used a bus seat to make her stand; Jackie Robinson used a baseball bat.

To continue her late husband's legacy, Rachel set up the Jackie Robinson Foundation. Through the years the foundation has helped students attend college who might not otherwise have been able to because they lacked the money to do so. In 2006, for instance, the foundation helped more than fifty needy students gain a college education.

Ed Charles, who played for the 1969 New York Mets championship team perhaps best expresses the impact Jackie Robinson made on people. As a twelve-year-old living in Daytona Beach, Florida, Charles saw Robinson play baseball during spring training. The excitement that coursed through him and other black youths of the late 1940s was something they still recalled thirty years later.

> Everybody in our part of town wanted to see him. Old people and small children, invalids and town drunks all walked through the streets. Some people were on crutches, and some blind people clutched the arms of friends, walking slowly on parade to that ball park to sit in the segregated section. We watched him play that day and finally believed what we had read in the papers, that one of us was out there on that ball field. When the game was over, we kids followed Jackie as he walked with his teammates to the train station, and when the train pulled out, we ran down the tracks listening for the sounds as far as we could. And when we finally couldn't hear it any longer, we ran some more and finally stopped and put our ears to the

---

Forgetting a Hero

In the spring of 1986 a reporter asked Vince Coleman, a black ballplayer with the St. Louis Cardinals, who Jackie Robinson was. "I don't know nothing about no Jackie Robinson," responded the major league ballplayer. One of Robinson's teammates, Joe Black, read a newspaper article about the incident and decided to send Coleman a letter. The thought of subsequent generations of black athletes knowing little of Jackie Robinson haunted Black.

> Vince, Jackie Robinson was more than an athlete. He was a man. Jackie Robinson stood alone as he challenged and integrated modern-day Major League baseball. His task was not easy nor quick. He suffered many mental and physical hurts. He accepted and overcame the slings, slams and insults so that young black youths, such as you, could dream of playing Major League baseball.

Maury Allen, *Jackie Robinson: A Life Remembered.* New York: Franklin Watts, 1987, pp. 12–13.

On April 15, 2006, New York Mets general manager Omar Minaya and Mets manager Willie Randolph flank Rachael Robinson during annual Jackie Robinson Day ceremonies at Shea Stadium.

tracks so we could feel the vibrations of that train carrying Jackie Robinson. We wanted to be part of him as long as we could."[105]

Because of Jackie Robinson, Charles wound up in the major leagues. Other young people, black and white, saw that with effort and dedication, anything was possible. Of all the accomplishments recorded by the Hall of Famer, that may be his most enduring feat.

Notes

Introduction: "All We Ask Is to Be Treated Fairly"

1. Quoted in Carl T. Rowan with Jackie Robinson, *Wait Till Next Year: The Life Story of Jackie Robinson*. New York: Random House, 1960, p. 24.

2. Quoted in John B. Holway, *Black Diamonds: Life in the Negro Leagues from the Men Who Lived It*. Westport, CT: Meckler, 1989, p. 60.

3. Quoted in Mark Ribowsky, *A Complete History of the Negro Leagues, 1884 to 1955*. New York: Citadel, 2002, p. 23.

4. Quoted in Ribowsky, *A Complete History of the Negro Leagues*, p. 85.

5. Quoted in Robert Peterson, *Only the Ball Was White*. Englewood Cliffs, NJ: Prentice-Hall, 1970, pp. 31–32.

6. Quoted in Donn Rogosin, *Invisible Men: Life in Baseball's Negro Leagues*. New York: Atheneum, 1983, p. 181.

7. Quoted in Ribowsky, *A Complete History of the Negro Leagues*, p. 252.

8. Quoted on the Official Site of Jackie Robinson. www.jackierobinson.com/about/quotes.html.

Chapter 1: "You Watched the White Kids Splash Around"

9. Quoted in Arnold Rampersad, *Jackie Robinson: A Biography*. New York: Alfred A. Knopf, 1997, p. 25.

10. Quoted in Rampersad, *Jackie Robinson: A Biography*, p. 15.

11. Jackie Robinson, as told to Alfred Duckett, *I Never Had It Made*. New York: G.P. Putnam's Sons, 1972, p. 16.

12. Quoted in Rowan with Robinson, *Wait Till Next Year*, p. 20.

13. Robinson and Duckett, *I Never Had It Made*, pp. 16–17.

14. Quoted in Rowan with Robinson, *Wait Till Next Year*, p. 23.

15. Quoted in David Falkner, *Great Time Coming*. New York: Simon & Schuster, 1995, p. 24.

16. Quoted in Rampersad, *Jackie Robinson: A Biography*, p. 24.

17. Robinson and Duckett, *I Never Had It Made*, p. 18.

18. Quoted in Rampersad, *Jackie Robinson: A Biography*, p. 35.

19. Quoted in Rowan with Robinson, *Wait Till Next Year*, p. 32.

20. Quoted in Falkner, *Great Time Coming*, p. 29.

21. Quoted in Falkner, *Great Time Coming*, p. 23.

22. Quoted in Rampersad, *Jackie Robinson: A Biography*, p. 39.

23. Quoted in Rampersad, *Jackie Robinson: A Biography*, p. 38.

Chapter 2: Trying to Fit In

24. Quoted in Falkner, *Great Time Coming*, p. 48.

25. Quoted in Falkner, *Great Time Coming*, p. 43.

26. Quoted in Rampersad, *Jackie Robinson: A Biography*, p. 57.

27. Quoted in Rampersad, *Jackie Robinson: A Biography*, p. 44.

28. Jackie Robinson, as told to Wendell Smith, *Jackie Robinson: My Own Story*. New York: Greenberg Publishers, 1948, p. 9.

29. Quoted in Rampersad, *Jackie Robinson: A Biography*, pp. 51–52.

30. Quoted in Rampersad, *Jackie Robinson: A Biography*, p. 55.

31. Robinson and Smith, *Jackie Robinson: My Own Story*, pp. 9–10.

32. Robinson and Smith, *Jackie Robinson: My Own Story*, p. 10.

33. Quoted in Rampersad, *Jackie Robinson: A Biography*, p. 78.

34. Quoted in Rowan with Robinson, *Wait Till Next Year*, p. 66.

35. Quoted in Maury Allen, *Jackie Robinson: A Life Remembered*. New York: Franklin Watts, 1987, p. 37.

Chapter 3: "Too Bad He's the Wrong Color"

36. Quoted in Rampersad, *Jackie Robinson: A Biography*, p. 90.

37. Quoted in Rampersad, *Jackie Robinson: A Biography*, p. 91.

38. Robinson and Duckett, *I Never Had It Made*, p. 28.

39. Quoted in Rowan with Robinson, *Wait Till Next Year*, p. 74.

40. Quoted in Rowan with Robinson, *Wait Till Next Year*, pp. 72–73.

41. Robinson and Duckett, *I Never Had It Made*, pp. 27–28.

42. Quoted in Rowan with Robinson, *Wait Till Next Year*, pp. 77–78.

43. Quoted in Rowan with Robinson, *Wait Till Next Year*, p. 83.

44. Robinson and Duckett, *I Never Had It Made*, p. 35.

45. Quoted in Rampersad, *Jackie Robinson: A Biography*, p. 120.

46. Quoted in Rampersad, *Jackie Robinson: A Biography*, p. 120.

47. Quoted in Falkner, *Great Time Coming*, p. 93.

Chapter 4: "Guts Not to Fight Back"

48. Quoted in Falkner, *Great Time Coming*, p. 106.

49. Quoted in Rampersad, *Jackie Robinson: A Biography*, p. 126.

50. Quoted in Robinson and Duckett, *I Never Had It Made*, p. 43.

51. Quoted in Robinson and Duckett, *I Never Had It Made*, p. 44.

52. Quoted in Robinson and Duckett, *I Never Had It Made*, p. 45.

53. Quoted in Robinson and Duckett, *I Never Had It Made*, p. 46.

54. Quoted in Robinson and Duckett, *I Never Had It Made*, p. 46.

55. Quoted in Falkner, *Great Time Coming*, p. 116.

56. Quoted in Falkner, *Great Time Coming*, p. 118.

57. Quoted in Falkner, *Great Time Coming*, p. 121.

58. Robinson and Duckett, *I Never Had It Made*, p. 54.

59. Quoted in Rampersad, *Jackie Robinson: A Biography*, p. 137.

60. Quoted in Rampersad, *Jackie Robinson: A Biography*, p. 138.

61. Quoted in Allen, *Jackie Robinson: A Life Remembered*, p. 79.

62. Robinson and Duckett, *I Never Had It Made*, p. 59.

63. Quoted in Robinson and Duckett, *I Never Had It Made*, p. 59.

64. Quoted in Rampersad, *Jackie Robinson: A Biography*, p. 154.

65. Robinson and Duckett, *I Never Had It Made*, p. 62.

66. Robinson and Duckett, *I Never Had It Made*, pp. 59–60.

67. Robinson and Duckett, *I Never Had It Made*, p. 64.

68. Quoted in Robinson and Duckett, *I Never Had It Made*, p. 65.

69. Quoted in Rampersad, *Jackie Robinson: A Biography*, p. 155.

Chapter 5: "Well, You Made It"

70. Quoted in Roger Kahn, *The Boys of Summer*. New York: Harper & Row, 1971, p. 323.

71. Quoted in Robinson and Smith, *Jackie Robinson: My Own Story*, p. 124.

72. Carl Erskine with Burton Rocks, *What I Learned from Jackie Robinson*. New York: McGraw-Hill, 2005, pp. 19–20.

73. Rachel Robinson with Lee Daniels, *Jackie Robinson: An Intimate Portrait*. New York: Harry N. Abrams, 1996, p. 66.

74. Rachel Robinson with Daniels, *Jackie Robinson: An Intimate Portrait*, p. 70.

75. Quoted in Robinson and Duckett, *I Never Had It Made*, p. 71.

76. Robinson and Duckett, *I Never Had It Made*, p. 72.

77. Quoted in Robinson and Duckett, *I Never Had It Made*, p. 73.

78. Quoted in Robinson and Duckett, *I Never Had It Made*, p. 75.

79. Quoted in Rachel Robinson with Daniels, *Jackie Robinson: An Intimate Portrait*, p. 75.

80. Quoted in Kahn, *The Boys of Summer*, p. 325.

81. Quoted in Robinson and Smith, *Jackie Robinson: My Own Story*, pp. 148–49.

82. Robinson and Duckett, *I Never Had It Made*, p. 77.

83. Quoted in Robinson and Smith, *Jackie Robinson: My Own Story*, pp. 146–47.

84. Quoted in Robinson and Smith, *Jackie Robinson: My Own Story*, pp. 149–50.

85. Quoted in Sharon Robinson, *Stealing Home*. New York: HarperCollins, 1996, p. 16.

86. Red Barber, *1947: When All Hell Broke Loose in Baseball*. Garden City, NY: Doubleday, 1982, p. 304.

87. Robinson and Duckett, *I Never Had It Made*, p. 81.

88. Rachel Robinson with Daniels, *Jackie Robinson: An Intimate Portrait*, p. 66.

Chapter 6: "We Wanted to Be Part of Him"

89. Quoted in Kahn, *The Boys of Summer*, p. 325.

90. Robinson and Duckett, *I Never Had It Made*, p. 12.

91. Quoted in Allen, *Jackie Robinson: A Life Remembered*, pp. 166–67.

92. Quoted in Kahn, *The Boys of Summer*, p. 315.

93. Quoted in Allen, *Jackie Robinson: A Life Remembered*, p. 164.

94. Quoted in Allen, *Jackie Robinson: A Life Remembered*, p. 237.

95. Erskine and Rocks, *What I Learned from Jackie Robinson*, p. 150.

96. Quoted in Glenn Stout and Dick Johnson, *Jackie Robinson: Between the Baselines*. San Francisco: Woodford, 1997, p. 182.

97. Quoted in Stout and Johnson, *Jackie Robinson: Between the Baselines*, p. 189.

98. Rachel Robinson with Daniels, *Jackie Robinson: An Intimate Portrait*, p. 201.

99. Quoted in Allen, *Jackie Robinson: A Life Remembered*, p. 231.

100. Quoted in Allen, *Jackie Robinson: A Life Remembered*, p. 5.

101. Rachel Robinson with Daniels, *Jackie Robinson: An Intimate Portrait*, p. 216.

102. Quoted in Allen, *Jackie Robinson: A Life Remembered*, p. 180.

103. Quoted in Falkner, *Great Time Coming*, p. 124.

104. Quoted in Allen, *Jackie Robinson: A Life Remembered*, p. 12.

105. Quoted in Allen, *Jackie Robinson: A Life Remembered*, p. 4.

Timeline

1919 Jackie Roosevelt Robinson is born in Cairo, Georgia, on January 31.

1920 Mallie Robinson leaves Georgia in May with her five children and resettles in Pasadena, California.

1937 Jackie Robinson enrolls at Pasadena Junior College.

1939 Robinson enrolls at the University of California, Los Angeles (UCLA).

1942 Robinson is drafted into the army on April 3.

1943 Robinson is commissioned as a second lieutenant in January.

1944 Robinson receives an honorable discharge from the military.

1945 The Brooklyn Dodgers announce they have signed Jackie Robinson.

1946 Robinson and Rachel Isum marry in February; their first child, Jackie Robinson Jr., is born in November.

1947 *Sporting News* names Robinson as the National League Rookie of the Year.

1948 Robinson participates in the filming of the movie *The Jackie Robinson Story*, which hits theaters in 1950.

1949 Robinson is named the National League's Most Valuable Player.

1956 Robinson retires from baseball to take a job with Chock Full o' Nuts; Robinson receives the NAACP's Spingarn Medal.

1962 Robinson is inducted into the Baseball Hall of Fame on July 23.

1971 Jackie Jr. is killed in an automobile accident.

1972 The Dodgers retire Robinson's uniform number, 42, in June; four months later, on October 24, Jackie Robinson dies.

For Further Reading

Books

Mark Alvarez, *The Official Baseball Hall of Fame Story of Jackie Robinson*. New York: Simon & Schuster, 1990. The author presents an excellent survey for young readers that covers every important aspect of Robinson's life.

William Brashler, *The Story of Negro League Baseball*. New York: Ticknor & Fields, 1994. This book provides a helpful examination of the origins and contributions of black baseball and the men who played it. Numerous photographs complement a fine text.

Carl Erskine with Burton Rocks, *What I Learned from Jackie Robinson*. New York: McGraw-Hill, 2005. A valuable memoir of this epochal time in baseball written by a baseball player who witnessed it. Erskine provides great insight into Robinson and his impact.

Wilmer Fields, *My Life in the Negro Leagues*. Westport, CT: Meckler, 1992. A player in the 1940s, Fields describes his days with the Homestead Grays and other Negro teams.

John B. Holway, *Blackball Stars: Negro League Pioneers*. Westport, CT: Meckler, 1988. Holway has compiled a superb collection of brief biographies of Negro league players, including Oscar Charleston and John Henry Lloyd.

————, *Black Diamonds: Life in the Negro Leagues from the Men Who Lived It*. Westport, CT: Meckler, 1989. John Holway has spent much of his life collecting stories from the men who played in black baseball. His contributions to the game's history have been unrivaled by any author. This fascinating book contains the reminiscences of eleven black stars. Along with Holway's other fine books, a reader will gain insight into the life and talents of these underappreciated men.

————, *Voices from the Great Black Baseball Leagues*. New York: Dodd, Mead, 1975. Holway's initial contribution to Negro baseball remains as valuable today as it was thirty years ago. In the book, he interviews eighteen major stars from those long-ago days.

Brent Kelley, *"I Will Never Forget": Interviews with 39 Former Negro League Players*. Jefferson, NC: McFarland, 2003. Kelley has devoted his career to capturing the stories of Negro League players. This book contains thirty-nine interviews, mostly dealing with the era following Jackie Robinson.

————, *Voices from the Negro Leagues*. Jefferson, NC: McFarland, 1998. Kelley interviewed fifty-two players from the Negro Leagues to compile this useful volume of oral history.

Patricia C. McKissack and Frederick McKissack Jr., *Black Diamond: The Story of the Negro Baseball Leagues*. New York: Scholastic, 1994. The authors have written a fine summary of the black baseball leagues. The chapters on the origins of black baseball and on playing in Latin America are particularly good.

Buck O'Neil, with Steve Wulf and David Conrads, *I Was Right on Time*. New York: Simon & Schuster, 1996. A great player in his own right, Buck O'Neil offers insights and commentary on black baseball and on the talented stars who performed in the days of separate leagues.

Satchel Paige, *Maybe I'll Pitch Forever*. Lincoln: University of Nebraska Press, 1993. Paige's colorful account of his life almost matches the colorfulness of his career. This autobiography is indispensable for obtaining an understanding of Paige and of black baseball.

Robert Peterson, *Only the Ball Was White*. Englewood Cliffs, NJ: Prentice Hall, 1970. Peterson broke new ground with his heralded history of the Negro Leagues. His book, the first of its type, explored the origins and impact of black baseball. He also includes a large section containing brief biographies of some of the most prominent black players.

Mark Ribowsky, *A Complete History of the Negro Leagues: 1884 to 1955*. New York: Citadel, 2002. Ribowsky has written a very thorough history of black baseball in the United States.

The narrative slows when he focuses on the business and political moves by team owners, but he compensates by including many fascinating anecdotes.

James A. Riley, *The Negro Leagues*. Philadelphia: Chelsea House, 1997. Junior high school students will enjoy Riley's survey of the Negro Leagues. The author explains black baseball from its origins to 1960.

Jackie Robinson, as told to Alfred Duckett, *I Never Had It Made*. New York: G.P. Putnam's Sons, 1972. This memoir of Jackie Robinson provides a superb vantage from which to examine the events of his life. The readable text is filled with illuminating anecdotes.

Jackie Robinson, as told to Wendell Smith, *Jackie Robinson: My Own Story*. New York; Greenberg, 1948. This book, written in cooperation with newspaper reporter Wendell Smith, was written one year after Robinson broke the color barrier. It offers insight and events that other books overlook or slight.

Rachel Robinson with Lee Daniels, *Jackie Robinson: An Intimate Portrait*. New York: Harry N. Abrams, 1996. The wife of Jackie Robinson has produced a remarkable examination of her husband. Much information exists here that can be obtained nowhere else.

Sharon Robinson, *Stealing Home*. New York: HarperCollins, 1996. Jackie Robinson's daughter offers a gripping look at the man she knew as father first and baseball player second. It contains many illuminating anecdotes.

Donn Rogosin, *Invisible Men: Life in Baseball's Negro Leagues*. New York: Atheneum, 1983. This is one of the finest histories of life in black baseball. Rogosin's chapters of life on the road, playing baseball in Latin America, and the march toward integration are particularly interesting.

Art Rust Jr., *"Get That Nigger Off the Field!"* New York: Delacorte, 1976. Rust's examination of black baseball yields numerous fascinating stories and revealing quotes. The author's background as a sports announcer helped prepare him for the task.

Glenn Stout and Dick Johnson, *Jackie Robinson: Between the Baselines*. San Francisco: Woodford, 1997. This outstanding book surveys Robinson's life and his impact on baseball. Essays by famous baseball writers are interspersed among the many photographs and the rich text.

Web Sites

Branch Rickey (www.baseballlibrary. com /baseballlibrary/ballplayers /R/Rickey_Branch.stm). This Web site focuses on Branch Rickey's role in baseball, including bringing Jackie Robinson into the major leagues.

Jackie Robinson: A Baseball Celebration (www.nytimes.com/specials/base ball/robinson-index.html). This site contains many articles about Jackie Robinson and audio interviews by associates, including Jackie's wife Rachel, Hank Aaron, and Duke Snider.

Jackie Robinson Foundation (www. jackierobinson.org). This is the official Web site for the educational foundation established by Robinson's wife, Rachel, in 1973. Much information exists at this site, including material on obtaining college scholarships and information about Jackie Robinson.

National Baseball Hall of Fame and Museum (www.baseballhalloffame. org). Anyone interested in the history of baseball, including Jackie Robinson's role, should consult this official Web site of baseball's Hall of Fame in Cooperstown, New York. Hundreds of brief accounts, profiles, and tons of statistics exist here.

Negro Leagues Legacy (http://mlb.mlb. com/NASApp/mlb/mlb/history/mlb _negro_leagues.jsp). This Web site offers helpful information on the history of Negro Leagues and profiles of its many stars. The site also contains excellent audio interviews with black baseball players.

The Official Site of Jackie Robinson (www.jackierobinson.com/about/ quotes.html). This excellent site offers helpful information, numerous quotations, and photographs of the star.

Videos

Craig Davidson, producer and director, *There Was Always Sun Shining Someplace*, Refocus Films, 1984. Interviews with Cool Papa Bell, Judy Johnson, and Monte Irvin make this documentary unique. James Earl Jones provides the narration.

Alfred E. Green, director, *The Jackie Robinson Story*. This 1950 Hollywood version of Robinson's life stars Jackie Robinson as himself and actress Ruby Dee as Rachel Robinson.

WTTW Chicago, *Only the Ball Was White*, 1992. Paul Winfield narrates this videotape about Negro League baseball. The production includes interviews of greats such as Satchel Paige, Buck Leonard, and David Malarcher.

Index

Picture Credits

About the Author

John F. Wukovits is a retired junior high school teacher and writer from Trenton, Michigan, who specializes in history and biography. Besides biographies of Anne Frank, Jim Carrey, Michael J. Fox, Stephen King, and Martin Luther King Jr. for Lucent, he has written biographies of the World War II commander Admiral Clifton Sprague, Barry Sanders, Tim Allen, Jack Nicklaus, Vince Lombardi, and Wyatt Earp. He is also the author of many books about World War II, including the July 2003 book *Pacific Alamo: The Battle for Wake Island*, the August 2006 *One Square Mile of Hell: The Battle for Tarawa*, and the November 2006 *Eisenhower: A Biography*. A graduate of the University of Notre Dame, Wukovits is the father of three daughters—Amy, Julie, and Karen—and the grandfather of Matthew, Megan, and Emma.